AMERICAN SPEECH

A Quarterly of Linguistic Usage

Volume 98, Number 1, February 2023

QUEER AND TRANS DIALECTOLOGY: EXPLORING
THE INTERSECTIONALITY OF REGIONALITY
edited by BRYCE McCLEARY *and* TYLER KIBBEY

T0371919

ONLINE ACCESS TO *AMERICAN SPEECH*

All *American Speech* content is available online in the form of enhanced PDFs, which are identical to the print pages but with added color, hyperlinks, and embedded audio and video files. (Note, embedded media may not be supported by all PDF viewers; if you are unable to access it using your current viewer, try opening the PDF in Adobe's free Acrobat Reader, http://get.adobe.com/reader/.) ADS members and institutions subscribing to the online version of *American Speech* can access journal content at https://read.dukeupress.edu/american-speech. If your institution subscribes to the online version, you can access journal content from any computer with an IP address registered to your institution or by entering remotely through a library gateway or VPN client. ADS members not affiliated with a subscribing institution will be asked to log in using their username and password. If you have not already set up a username and password, you can create an online account with your customer number, found on the mailing label on your paper copy of *American Speech*. If you have not kept your mailing labels, you can contact Duke University Press customer service at subscriptions@dukeupress.edu or 888-651-0122, Monday–Friday, 8:30–4:30 EST/EDT.

AUDIO FEATURES

The online version of some issues also contain a downloadable audio feature on a subject of interest to readers of *American Speech*, such as interviews with notable linguists, documentary-style treatments of dialect or sociolinguistic variation, compilations of field recordings, and so on. The audio feature's title and creator(s) are included in the issue's table of contents, and an abstract, reference list, and author bio appear in the pages of the print version. For more information, see "Audio Features: New Sounds of *American Speech*" (*American Speech* 87, no. 1 [Spring 2012]: 3–6; https://doi.org/10.1215/00031283-1599932). Readers can access the sound file by following the directions above for online access. Prospective contributors should submit a detailed proposal, including a synopsis of the piece; an outline that further particularizes the synopsis, with estimated timings of each component; and a description of the facilities available to produce an audio presentation of professional quality.

TEACHING AMERICAN SPEECH

Each May issue of *American Speech* contains an annual pedagogical section titled "Teaching American Speech," dedicated to the teaching of American speech in every relevant curricular venue, from elementary school to graduate school. Installments contain peer-reviewed full-length articles; brief notes on course construction, assignments, evaluation, resources, and techniques; and reviews of relevant texts. For more information, see "*American Speech*: The Mission" (*American Speech* 82, no. 3 [Fall 2007]: 231–34; https://doi.org/10.1215/00031283-2007-010). Submissions should be emailed to managing editor Charles Carson at american.speech@duke.edu or mailed to him at *American Speech*, Duke University Press, 905 W Main St Ste 18B, Durham NC 27701-2054.

EDITOR'S NOTE

American Speech turns 100 in two years (celebrating with other eminent cen-
tenarian journals, *Language* and *The New Yorker*). Since 1925, our journal,
explicitly or implicitly, has reported on dialects and languages connected to
groups of people residing in the Western Hemisphere. One interpretation of
the journal's topical scope has been the examination of "English in America"
(Algeo 2009, 196; see Picone 2022; Adams 2022). Indeed, articles have often
been published on varieties of English in the United States and Canada. Yet,
for the past 98 years, English has not been the only language exclusively reported on. The journal has published articles containing contributions that
appeal to a broad readership, including articles about the language behavior
of non-English varieties (see Bayley 2017, 2022; Salmons 2022). In some
spaces, research appearing in *American Speech* seems quite progressive. For
example, recently, the *New York Times* published an awareness-raising piece
by Simon Romero (2023) titled "New Mexico Is Losing a Form of Spanish
Spoken Nowhere Else on Earth"; interestingly, 26 years prior, Garland Bills
(1997) described the grammatical characteristics of this rare New Mexican
Spanish variety.

An example of the journal's past and present scope has been to cover
variations connected to specific social groups. Since the current issue presents
four papers investigating how LGBTQ+ identity intersects with geography
and this issue's "Among the New Words" feature complements such research
by covering words related to gender identity, I searched for *gay* in *American
Speech*, both on JSTOR (1925–99) and the Duke University Press (2000–)
sites. Presumably, a longstanding LBTQ+ term with an early 1922 entry in
the *OED* coinciding with the founding of *American Speech* could demonstrate
the degree to which the journal has published research on the topic over its
tenure. Before 2000, when Duke Press took over publishing *American Speech*,
there were few articles, but 10 or so between 1980 and 1999 to keep one
glancing at the appropriate lexical items. In over two decades of the Duke
University Press era, *American Speech* published two special issues, the first
one being "Sociophonetics and Sexuality" (2011), edited by Rob Podesva
and Penny Eckert (2011), and the present one, edited by Bryce McCleary
and Tyler Kibbey. In addition to the articles in these special issues, studies
explore the relationship between gender identity and geography or speech
communities (Battistella 2006; Levon 2006; Campbell-Kibler 2007; Zimmer,
Solomon, and Carson 2014; Lo Vecchio 2022).

Over the past few years, articles appearing within our covers indicate
a change in our conception of what the field of dialectology can cover.
I anticipate this trend continuing well beyond my tenure at the journal. One

American Speech, Vol. 98, No. 1, February 2023   DOI 10.1215/00031283-10579416

primary driver in the direction of our journal, and other academic journals, is the interest of researchers conducting investigations and submitting those reports for publication. This issue's particular topic exploring identities and regions is a part of the forward-looking vision for the journal. *American Speech* will seek to publish more articles like these in the next 100 years.

To that end, the committee on the 100th anniversary of *American Speech* (myself, Katie Carmichael, Charles Carson, Connie Eble, Natalie Schilling, and Jessi Grieser) met during the recent American Dialect Society annual convention in Denver and discussed where we might take the journal during the year. The goal is to run the four issues of our first triple-digit volume as special thematic issues. Topically, the articles we seek include work on the dialectology of people indigenous to the Americas, people with ancestry to past enslavement, or groups connected to non-European ancestry. Also, the committee primarily seeks research covering varieties of the Americas outside the United States within the Western Hemisphere (including appropriate islands in the Pacific and Atlantic Oceans). All manuscripts may cover a range of dialectological work, especially geography, group affiliation, lexicography, onomastics, substrate effects, and grammatical, sociohistorical, and sociophonetic variation. Authors wishing to contribute to this volume are invited to send me an extended abstract of their proposed article or submit their article (if already written) through the journal's ScholarOne portal. For inclusion in a relevant issue, final versions of the manuscripts should be received by mid-2024, depending on the research topic.

Now I want to warmly express my gratitude to everyone who made the success of *American Speech* possible. Associate editors include Alexandra D'Arcy (Univ. of Victoria), audio features; Katie Carmichael (Virginia Polytechnic Institute and State Univ.), book reviews; and Jeff Reaser (North Carolina State Univ.), pedagogical section. Journal leadership will examine an ensuing editorial succession process in the next two years. The past two editors held decade-long terms, and my decade as editor will coincide with the centennial, making 2025 or 2026 a good transition year. Leading up to this transformative point, we may restructure the coverage of these associate editor positions, for example, combining the audio features, curated collections, and special issues into a single editorial role.

I especially want to thank scholars who served on the Editorial Advisory Committee during 2021 and 2022. Committee members continue to affirm the value of our work: Michael Adams (Indiana Univ.), Gabriela Alfaraz (Michigan State Univ.), David Bowie (Univ. of Alaska Anchorage), Elaine Chun (Univ. of South Carolina), Anne Curzan (Univ. of Michigan), Derek Denis (Univ. of Toronto Mississauga), Betsy Evans (Univ. of Washington), Shelome Gooden (Univ. of Pittsburgh), Jessica Grieser (Univ. of Michigan),

Jack Grieve (Univ. of Birmingham), Lauren Hall-Lew (Univ. of Edinburgh), J. Daniel Hasty (Coastal Carolina Univ.), Nicole Holliday (Pomona College), Sonja Lanehart (Univ. of Arizona), Joseph Salmons (Univ. of Wisconsin–Madison), Sali Tagliamonte (Univ. of Toronto), Erik Thomas (North Carolina State Univ.), and Jim Wood (Yale Univ.).

Moreover, we can now make visible the invaluable readers who have evaluated manuscripts for *American Speech* and PADS for the last two years, those who evaluated manuscripts for publication-worthiness and provide recommendations for authors. These kind readers include: Lamont Antieau (Univ. of Kentucky), Salvatore Attardo (Texas A&M Univ.), Dennis Baron (Univ. of Illinois at Urbana-Champaign), Rusty Barrett (Univ. of Kentucky), Kara Becker (Reed College), Erica Benson (Univ. of Wisconsin–Eau Claire), Charles Boberg (McGill Univ.), Paulina Bounds (Tennessee Technical Univ.), Josh Brown (Univ. of Wisconsin–Eau Claire), Rachel Burdin (Univ. of New Hampshire), Becky Childs (James Mason Univ.), Tracy Conner (Northwestern Univ.), Jennifer Cramer (Univ. of Kentucky), Aaron Dinkin (San Diego State Univ.), Marianna Di Paolo (Univ. of Utah), Stan Dubinsky (Univ. of South Carolina), Charlie Farrington (Virginia Polytechnic Institute and State Univ.), Jon Forrest (Univ. of Georgia), Kirk Hazen (Univ. of West Virginia), Benjamin Hebblethwaite (Univ. of Florida), Larry Horn (Yale Univ.), Bill Idsardi (Univ. of Maryland), Steve Keiser (Marquette Univ.), Scott Kiesling (Univ. of Pittsburgh), Sharese King (Univ. of Chicago), Mary Kohn (Kansas State Univ.), Wesley Leonard (Univ. of California, Riverside), Stephen Levey (Univ. of Ottawa), Bryce McCleary (Rice Univ.), Lisa Minnick (Western Michigan Univ.), Monica Nesbitt (Indiana Univ.), Jen Nycz (Georgetown Univ.), Laura Patterson (Open Univ.), Mark Pierce (Univ. of Texas), Robin Queen (Univ. of Michigan), Eric Ramy (Univ. of Wisconsin–Madison), Kate Remlinger (Grand Valley State Univ.), Julie Roberts (Univ. of Vermont), Natalie Schilling (Georgetown Univ.), Krystal Smalls (Univ. of Illinois Urbana-Champaign), Hiram Smith (Bucknell Univ.), Arthur Spears (City Univ. of New York), Lauren Squires (Ohio State Univ.), Jim Stanford (Dartmouth College), Joey Stanley (Brigham Young Univ.), Abby Walker (Virginia Polytechnic Institute and State Univ.), James Walker (La Trobe Univ.), Anja Wanner (Univ. of Wisconsin–Madison), Rebecca Wheeler (Christopher Newport Univ.), Raffaella Zanuttini (Yale Univ.), and Lynn Zhang (Univ. of Wisconsin–Madison).

Many thanks to the word crowd producing our "Among the New Words" feature, specifically Benjamin Zimmer (*Wall Street Journal*), Kelly Wright (Virginia Polytechnic Institute and State Univ.), Brianne Hughes (Wordnik), and Charles Carson (Duke Univ. Press). Lynn Zhang (Univ. of Wisconsin–Madison), Jaidan McLean (Univ. of Oregon), and Kate Whitcomb

(*Layman's Linguist*) provided assistance in the collection of citations. Seth Rosenblatt (*The Parallax*) consulted on the cybersecurity installment. Also pitching in were individual entry writers Emily Brewster (Merriam-Webster Inc.), Dominique Canning (Univ. of Michigan), Katie Carmichael (Virginia Polytechnic Institute and State Univ.), Kirby Conrod (Swarthmore College), Nancy Friedman (*Fritinancy*), Jessica Grieser (Univ. of Michigan), Nicole Holliday (Pomona College), Sonja Lanehart (Univ. of Arizona), Ayesha Malik (independent scholar), Mark Peters (independent scholar), Jane Solomon (Emojipedia), and Lynn Zhang (Univ. of Wisconsin–Madison).

Rob Dilworth's patience and Duke University Press's support are very much appreciated year in and year out. This journal cannot work without Charles Carson's detailed contribution to our articles' quality and packaging of the journal graphics, and he does far more than merely manage the journal. Finally, I thank Lynn Zhang for working with me on *American Speech* for two years as my project assistant, sponsored by the Department of English, University of Wisconsin–Madison.

REFERENCES

Adams, Michael. 2022. "ADS, the Society's Dictionary, and Anglocentrism." *American Speech* 97, no. 1 (Feb.): 30–35. https://doi.org/10.1215/00031283-9616175.

Algeo, John. 2009. *The Origins and Development of the English Language.* 6th ed. Boston: Thomson Wadsworth.

Battistella, Edwin. 2006. "Girly Men and Girly Girls." *American Speech* 81, no. 1 (Spring): 100–110. https://doi.org/10.1215/00031283-2006-006.

Bayley, Robert. 2017. "Presidential Address: Dialectology in a Multilingual America." *American Speech* 92, no. 1 (Feb.): 6–22. https://doi.org/10.1215/00031283-4153175.

Bayley, Robert. 2022. "Acknowledging Our Multilingual Reality." *American Speech* 97, no. 1 (Feb.): 40–43. https://doi.org/10.1215/00031283-9616197.

Bills, Garland D. 1997. "New Mexican Spanish: Demise of the Earliest European Variety in the United." *American Speech* 72, no. 2 (Summer): 154–71. https://doi.org/10.2307/455787.

Campbell-Kibler, Kathryn. 2007. "Accent, (ing), and the Social Logic of Listener Perceptions." *American Speech* 82, no. 1 (Spring): 32–64. https://doi.org/10.1215/00031283-2007-002.

Levon, Erez. 2006. "Teasing Apart to Bring Together: Gender and Sexuality in Variationist Research." *American Speech* 86, no. 1 (Spring): 69–84. https://doi.org/10.1215/00031283-1277519.

Lo Vecchio, Nicholas. 2022. "Revisiting *berdache*: Notes on a Translinguistic Lexical Creation." *American Speech* 97, no. 3 (Aug.): 345–73. https://doi.org/10.1215/00031283-9616142.

Picone, Michael D. 2022. "Just What Is 'American Speech' Anyway?" *American Speech* 97, no. 1 (Feb.): 5–30. https://doi.org/10.1215/00031283-9616164.

Podesva, Robert J., and Penelope Eckert, eds. 2011. "Sociophonetics and Sexuality." Special issue, *American Speech* 86, no. 1 (Spring). https://read.dukeupress.edu/american-speech/issue/86/1.

Romero, Simon. 2023. "New Mexico Is Losing a Form of Spanish Spoken Nowhere Else on Earth." *New York Times*, Apr. 9, 2023. https://www.nytimes.com/2023/04/09/us/new-mexico-spanish.html.

Salmons, Joseph. 2022. "American Speech in Action: Policy versus Practice." *American Speech* 97, no. 1 (Feb.): 36–40. https://doi.org/10.1215/00031283-9616186.

Zimmer, Benjamin, Jane Solomon, and Charles E. Carson. 2014. "Among the New Words." *American Speech* 89, no. 4 (Winter): 470–96. https://doi.org/10.1215/00031283-2908233.

THOMAS PURNELL
University of Wisconsin–Madison

CULTURES AND COMPLEXITIES CONCERNING PLACE

BRYCE McCLEARY, *Rice University*
TYLER KIBBEY, *Humboldt-Universität zu Berlin*

This special issue of *American Speech* offers a survey of the ways that place, region, and community intersect in contemporary dialectology and socio-linguistics. It contributes to the body of scholarship on regional linguistic variation by complicating the notion of region and what that means for different communities at the many and complex intersections of gender and sexuality, along with other categories of identity. These articles include analyses of intersectional regionality in the identity construction of Okla-homa City drag queens, transnational divergence of nonbinary neologisms in Quebec French, queer language differentiation in Jewish-English-speaking communities in Seattle, and disciplinary constructions of researcher identity in contemporary American dialectology and its antecedents. Taken together, these articles represent a reconsideration of the role of place, region, and community within the context of gender, sexuality, and language.

This issue began in the height of the global pandemic, during which linguistics organizations like the Linguistic Society of America and the Associa-ção Brasileira de Lingüística launched digital series covering various aspects of linguistic research. Both of these organizations featured talks on various research in LGBTQ+ linguistics, and both of us took part in these series. In them, two ideas emerged: that queer and trans people had not been included in much dialectological work focused on region and that noncisgender and nonheterosexual experience can complicate and make complex the notions we have about place and region in sociolinguistics. These observations led to a call for research on the complexity and intersectionality of place within (socio-)linguistics and what that meant for LGBTQ+ speakers, and we are proud to say that the articles featured here do so in novel and important ways.

Bryce McCleary's article addresses a community of drag performers in Oklahoma City, in a historic site for LGBTQ+ communities in a city and state that are often hostile to such communities. Additionally, the participants describe this safe space and what it means for them as LGBTQ+ Oklaho-mans and as participants in drag culture in the city. The data are analyzed and found to highlight not only their awareness of language, place, and community (à la Preston 2010) but also their identities and experiences (e.g., Bucholtz and Hall 2008; Hall 2013) in the cultural landscape of the Oklahoma City drag scene. What emerges is a sense that diversity must be fought for even in such safe spaces, particularly along racial lines, and that competition for spotlight and success as a performer muddles the "safety"

American Speech, Vol. 98, No. 1, February 2023   DOI 10.1215/00031283-10579429

of such a space. Ultimately, however, this work finds that both language and community relationships/kinship play vital roles in navigating this interesting and often difficult cultural terrain.

Mireille Elchacar investigates terms used for nonbinary identities in Quebec French, an attempt to fill already-recognized gaps (e.g., Greco 2015; Lorenzi 2017; Elchacar and Salita 2018), addressing competing interests of identity-motivated terms and purism-motivated condemnation of such terms (i.e., in Remysen 2009). More specifically, the Quebec language institution, l'Office québécois de la langue française, opposed the growingly popular terms *LGBT** and *queer* because of its sensitive history with anglicisms. The study finds that noncisgender groups, who have been traditionally socially disadvantaged, gain symbolic power by opting for their own terms in the face of institutional pushback and in ways that connect LGBTQ+ Quebecois communities to a broader, global LGBTQ+ community.

Ellen Perleberg, Grace Elizabeth C. Dy, and Lindsay Hipp investigate Jewish queer community language in Seattle, also considering its spread from in-group community members to cis-heterosexual communities (as in Smorag 2008) in broader shared Jewish spaces. In view of the traditionally safe and welcoming region of Seattle for LGBTQ+ peoples, this study focuses on participants' experiences with queer Jewish language, a variety of Benor's (2009) concept of Jewish-English: how they learned it and how it interacts with identity practice along gender, sexuality, and cultural/religious lines. The observations suggest that queer community leaders may play a significant role in the popularity and spread of queer Jewish language in Seattle.

Tyler Kibbey examines the notion of rootedness (Reed 2016, 2020) as a metric for attachment to place and how, perhaps especially though not exclusively in the American South, belonging to place can be quite complicated. This counter-theoretical review considers the roles of the researcher's positionality and the speakers' agency as critical components needing to be addressed in a metric for rootedness. As such, this research explores the notions of security (or lack thereof) and community hostility as factors that might undermine measurements of belonging to a place.

All of these articles address the complexity of region for LGBTQ+ speakers. They all touch on notions of place, from the more localized situations to broader notions of region, as it intersects with identities and experiences. It is our hope that such research will be only part of a longer tradition in the nuanced inspection of the intersectionality of regionality. And we hope it will spark curiosity and questions concerning the ways that we study place—in both methodological considerations and analytic approaches to data—and what place can mean for underrepresented populations of speakers.

REFERENCES

Benor, Sarah Bunin. 2009. "Do American Jews Speak a 'Jewish Language'? A Model of Jewish Linguistic Distinctiveness." *Jewish Quarterly Review* 99, no. 2 (Spring): 230–69. https://doi.org/10.1353/jqr.0.0046.

Bucholtz, Mary, and Kira Hall. 2008. "All of the Above: New Coalitions in Sociocultural Linguistics." In "Socio-cultural Linguistics," edited by Mary Bucholtz and Kira Hall. Special issue, *Journal of Sociolinguistics* 12, no. 4 (Sept.): 401–31. https://doi.org/10.1111/j.1467-9841.2008.00382.x.

Elchacar, Mireille, and Ada Luna Salita. 2018. "Les appellations des identités de genre non traditionnelles: Une approche lexicologique." *Langage et société*, no. 165, 139–65. https://doi.org/10.3917/ls.165.0139.

Greco, Luca. 2015. "Présentation: La fabrique des genres et ses sexualités." *Langage et société*, no. 152, 7–16. https://doi.org/10.3917/ls.152.0007.

Hall, Kira. 2013. "Commentary 1: 'It's a Hijra'! Queer Linguistics Revisited." *Discourse and Society* 24, no. 5 (Sept.): 634–42. https://doi.org/10.1177/0957926513490321.

Lorenzi, Marie-Émilie. 2017. "'Queer,' 'transpédégouine,' 'torduEs,' entre adaptation et réappropriation, les dynamiques de traduction au cœur des créations langagières de l'activisme féministe *queer*." *GLAD!*, no. 2. http://journals.open edition.org/glad/462.

Preston, Dennis R. 2010. "Language, People, Salience, Space: Perceptual Dialectology and Language Regard." *Dialectologia*, no. 5, 87–131. http://www.edicions .ub.edu/revistes/ejecuta_descarga.asp?codigo=642.

Reed, Paul E. 2016. "Sounding Appalachian: /aɪ/ Monophthongization, Rising Pitch Accents, and Rootedness." Ph.D. diss., University of South Carolina.

Reed, Paul E. 2020. "The Importance of Rootedness in the Study of Appalachian English: Case Study Evidence for a Proposed Rootedness Metric." *American Speech* 95, no. 2 (May): 203–26. https://doi.org/10.1215/00031283-7706532.

Remysen, Wim. 2009. "Description et évaluation de l'usage canadien dans les chroniques de langage: Contribution à l'étude de l'imaginaire linguistique des chroniqueurs canadiens-français." Ph.D. diss., Université Laval.

Smorag, Pascale. 2008. "From Closet Talk to PC Terminology : Gay Speech and the Politics of Visibility." *Transatlantica* 2008, no. 1: art. 3503. Association Française d'Études Américaines. https://doi.org/10.4000/transatlantica.3503.

"WE ALL COUNTRY": REGION, PLACE, AND COMMUNITY LANGUAGE AMONG OKLAHOMA CITY DRAG PERFORMERS

BRYCE McCLEARY

Rice University

ABSTRACT: This study aims to build on limited research in Oklahoma LGBTQ+ populations and to consider intersectional queer and trans perspectives on region and place as constructs within broader sociolinguistic work. The primary data come from linguistic ethnographic and queer folk linguistic work in a community of drag performers who detail the hardships of navigating a region like Oklahoma as nonheterosexual, noncisgender, and in some cases non-White Oklahomans. Their discussions of 39th Street, a culturally important site with a long history of LGBTQ+ protection, reveal that it, too, is riddled with racial, transphobic, and class-based ideologies that intersect with economic and practice-based difficulties for both new and seasoned performers. What emerges is an indication that queer kinship systems, familial communities within the community of practice, are integral parts of survival for performers and that language is both affected by such kinship systems and employed as a tool for navigating this place.

KEYWORDS: Oklahoma, queer folk linguistics, language regard, LGBTQ+ linguistics, queer kinship

REGION: OKLAHOMA AND THE SOUTHERN PERIPHERY

Oklahoma is an interesting site for the nuance and complexity often wrapped up with the construct of REGION in sociolinguistics, given that researchers who attempt to document language variation in the state find a fascinating mix of dialectal influences. One of those influences has undoubtedly been the South, including some varieties of Appalachian, or the Upper South (Southard 1993). The effects of the South and of the rural, often conservative culture in Oklahoma (frequently described in folk linguistic interviews as "country"; see Hall-Lew and Stephens 2012; McCleary 2016) has contributed to a number of sociolinguistic realities: Southernisms and participation in some Southern features; linguistic and cultural identification with the South (though not entirely; see Bakos 2013) and its effect on linguistic insecurity and stigmatization of dialects (McCleary 2016); and, most relevant to the

American Speech, Vol. 98, No. 1, February 2023   DOI 10.1215/00031283-10579442

present work, a history of discrimination against queer, trans, and LGBTQ2+ peoples (Bachhofer 2006). Rather than covering the long history of the construct of region and place in dialectology and sociolinguistics, this section offers a snapshot of the sociolinguistic and cultural history of Oklahoma.

The dialectological complexity of this region is in part a result of its relatively late statehood (1907), prior to which it was composed of the Indian and Oklahoma Territories. Large unceded tracts of these territories, the site of many sovereign tribal lands and allocated plots for the forced migration of many Southern tribes of Indigenous peoples, were eventually offered up by the U.S. government to any willing (mostly White) settlers in a series of land runs. Settlers came in seven land rushes, participating in the stealing of Native people's lands, from 1889 to 1901. Southard (1993) concludes that the majority of settlers came from the Midwest (which he divides into Lower and Upper Midwest), though a consistent input of Upper South settlers appears in every land run, as do smaller numbers of settlers from Texas and the Lower South.

This historically problematic but linguistically diverse mix of settlers contributes to the presence of linguistic features that would otherwise be regionally constrained. For example, the mix of Midlanders, Southerners, and Midwesterners to Oklahoma contributed to the lexical items such as *y'all* (Tillery and Bailey 1998); the Southern-associated PIN-PEN merger (Bailey, Tillery, and Wikle 1997; Weirich 2013); the Midwestern COT-CAUGHT merger (Bailey et al. 1993); and a mixture of both Midland and Southern phonetic variation (Thomas 2001; Labov, Ash, and Boberg 2006). This work has unfortunately not given equal attention Black, Indigenous, and other Oklahomans of color, who also contribute to the linguistic and cultural tapestry of the state and have also suffered in the problematic history of the state. Historically, many Indigenous peoples have been treated as second-class citizens and were often abused, and claims to sovereign tribal lands have been altogether ignored (e.g., Associated Press 2022). African Americans, many still enslaved, began entering the region back during the Trail of Tears (1830–50)(Chang 2010; Miles 2015) and have since endured a long history of oppression (Luckerson 2021). One of the state's most horrific examples of such cultures clashing is the Tulsa Race Massacre of 1921, in which innocent Black Oklahomans were attacked as a result of racial tensions and hearsay allegations. Such a diverse and complex sociocultural history is reflected in the sociolinguistic situation of Oklahoma today, especially for queer and trans people of color, even if much of this history has been left out of traditional regional dialectological work.

It should be noted that the phrasing of *queer and trans* occurs more than once in this article for two reasons. The first is that, though queer linguistics has always been interested in (non)normativity pertaining to gender and sexuality, some work in the subfield excludes or does not consider fully the trans experience as different from cisgender gay and lesbian experiences (Zimman 2020). Second, more recent work (e.g., L. Jones 2022) highlights the importance of listening to what trans individuals have to say about language and how they navigate linguistic violence (e.g., misgendering and misrepresentation), something an updated folk linguistic model should be better equipped for. Lastly, the designation of *queer and trans* for both the perspective taken on these data and the participants in this project is one of the ways this research tries to continue the trans linguistics goal of seeing trans people as "no longer objects to be evaluated for their implications to gender theories and politics developed by cis thinkers, but analytic agents with unique capacity to inform the discipline" (Zimman 2020).

Though very little sociolinguistic work on LGBTQ+ speakers has been conducted in Oklahoma, other historical and sociocultural accounts of some of the LGBTQ+ communities has been done. For example, Bachhofer (2006) reports that Oklahoma City had established a thriving underground community of gay and bisexual men by the 1960s, which was followed by years of police violence, heavy monitoring of gay-associated areas of the city, and state-sanctioned violence again queer Oklahomans. A liberation movement, paralleling those in larger U.S. cities in the 1970s, followed, which led to the establishment of a safe, protected area of the city known as the 39th Street enclave, a culturally and societally important safe space and the main site for Oklahoma City's drag performance scene. It should be noted, however, that Bachhofer (2006) is primarily interested in White gay and bisexual cisgender male subcultures. Outside of cisgender cultuer, Bachhofer touches very little on the experiences of lesbians, queer people of color, or noncisgender Oklahomans, which is a shame given how vital a role the lesbian, gender nonconforming, and trans communities have played in shaping of the 39th Street community and LGBTQ+ communities more broadly, especially drag communities (see Barrett 1999, 2017).

PLACE: OKLAHOMA CITY'S 39TH STREET ENCLAVE

This section introduces the discourse drag performers employ concerning the state, Oklahoma City, 39th Street, the drag scene specifically, and the language that permeates the area. Nearly all observations and recording sessions occurred on 39th Street, in what many locals refer to as "the Strip," "the Gayborhood," or historically "Glitter Alley." Most of the venues and stores in the area are still LGBTQ-owned, though various respondents commented on the fact that they are all owned by older, White cisgender men. It remains heavily trafficked, with nearly half a dozen venues for drag entertainment, an area with local norms that at times push back against broader regional ideologies and at other times embraces them.

This project drew from several approaches to linguistic ethnographic work (Copland and Creese 2015; Pérez-Milans 2016; Kvam 2017; Stofleth and Manusov 2019) and borrowed specifically the use of participants' descriptions of the community and their role within it to inform the types of questions asked in recorded interviews. The larger project from which these data came built on folk linguistic methodology (Niedzielski and Preston 2003), including a traditional focus on explicit (meta)language (e.g., Preston 1996) but with a specific focus on the implicata and presuppositional material within the discourse (see Preston 2019). Additionally, my personal approach to the data also employs the sociocultural methods in the study of identity in interaction (Bucholtz and Hall 2005, 2008). What resulted was a queered folk linguistics (McCleary, forthcoming) that uses folk linguistic data to inform regional/community language as well as to understand the varying ways speakers engage with language (in complex, intersectional ways) to do identity work. While the data of this present paper do not focus on the folk linguistic material, the same methods are applied, and the responses all stem from questions in the same recording sessions.

Even in its design, this research depends on in-group insight and community engagement, and it attempts to maintain an awareness of community and regional histories. It complicates the discussions of privilege and power in the community today and is used to better understand the community, especially in the motivations for particular language-related phenomena. To attempt such research more responsibly, the analysis has been informed by raciolinguistic methods in order to combat the biases of the researcher and more accurately relaying nuanced information in the data without furthering problems of racialization. That is, people (including linguists) often engage in racializing people based on certain cues, mapping or projecting a sense of ethnic difference onto racialized bodies (see Charity Hudley 2017; Rosa and Flores 2017; Smitherman 2017; Flores, Lewis, and Phuong 2018). Just as important, the language, slang, and performance among the members of this community are all heavily influenced by African American Language (AAL) features and styles, though they are not always credited with that sociolinguistic history. Thus, raciolinguistics is a necessarily implementation in this project, one that necessitates an incorporation of intersectionality (Carbado et al. 2013; Crenshaw 2016) as a critical component of socioculturally informed identity studies (e.g., Bucholtz 2018; Zentella 2018).

This article draws on nearly 10 hours of speech data from interviews and group discussions with six respondents, three of whom have around ten or more years of experience and three who are relative newcomers to Oklahoma City's drag circuit (see table 1). All respondents were a part of the larger queer folk linguistic project that asked about language regard, life, and experience in this community. The data for this article come primarily from questions about Oklahoma and drag in Oklahoma, the differences in venues on 39th Street, and the communities within the broader LGBTQ+ community of this area.

TALK ABOUT DRAG IN OKLAHOMA. Drag performance as a form of expression and entertainment has grown in popularity immensely in the last decade, having far-reaching effects on drag communities such as that in Oklahoma City. Every participant noted the widespread fandom of shows like *RuPaul's Drag Race* and social media–based drag performers. While there has likely always been an attitude that the next generation of drag performers are changing things, all local performers exhibit a complicated relationship with the spread of drag culture.

Wider exposure to drag adds to the pop-cultural relevance and, perhaps as a result, the value of drag artistic endeavors. It also pits local performers against big-budgets, Hollywood, and digital venues that can take away from the regionality of drag entertainment. Performers in Oklahoma frequently discuss the spread of drag culture, and they all offer characterizations of Oklahoma drag specifically as it is differentiated from an otherwise "mainstream" drag scene. In excerpt 1 below, Foxxi, a performer with over a decade of experience in the Oklahoma City drag circuit, references some of the defining characteristics of the local scene. When asked about the LGBTQ+ community in Oklahoma more broadly, Foxxi characterizes the entire group by saying, "We all country as hell I ain't gon lie, we are," an indication that, despite the many things that separate and differentiate the

TABLE 1
Participants' Experience, Age, and Self-Described Ethno-racial
and Gender Identities

Performer	Experience (years)	Age	Ethno-Racial Identity	Gender Identity (performer)
Kelly	19	41	Caucasian	male
Foxxi	10	31	African American	female
Gizele	9	30	Black	cis-male
Rae	2	30	Black/AA	transgender
Guin	<1	25	Caucasian	transgender woman
Alexander	>1	22	White	male

community, she sees an Okie-ness that brings many of the trans and queer community together.

Foxxi recalls her early experience in the Oklahoma City drag scene as "upscale" and "pretty and polished." These two concepts, class and beauty, both concern appearance and performance, but they are not the primary concerns of all performers in today's drag scene, something Foxxi only implies here with her label "old school drag" but on which she elaborates in excerpt 2. She characterizes Oklahoma drag today as still having some "old school" aesthetics, calling attention to "costumes," "big hair," and "stone," which correspond to tailored outfits, higher-quality wigs, and lots of jewels, respectively.

> Excerpt 1. Foxxi describing drag in Oklahoma ◄⑴ [1]
> INTERVIEWER: so how would you describe drag in Oklahoma
> FOXXI: ooh honey that's a long conversation too I mean Oklahoma drag has
>   changed ever since like I first saw drag I felt like it was more of the upscale
>   'cause you know you wanna be pretty you wanna be polished and together
>   which you should always wanna be but it was more it was like very old school
>   drag you know

Foxxi distinguishes "old school" Oklahoma drag from her own drag aesthetics by using terms like *ratchet* and *hood*, descriptors that index associations with African American culture and identity but also have class-based associations. *Ratchet* has been described as a word that indicates behavior deemed inappropriate in public, perhaps déclassé (Weinraub 2015). Both *ratchet* and *hood* are associated with the language of hip-hop music and culture (T. Jones 2015; Pichler and Williams 2016); note also that in the excerpt *ratchet* may be modifying *hood* to achieve a more specific description. Taylor Jones (2015) adds that these items have been "noticed" and then borrowed by the "white mainstream" (411) and is therefore not necessarily reliable as an indicator of speaker status regarding AAL varieties.

> Excerpt 2. Foxxi unpacking old school drag ◄⑴
> FOXXI: Oklahoma is very old school they want jewels they want costumes they
>   want big hair they want stone and that's fine but every person don't wanna
>   do that you know people wanna come out in a trash bag or a something–
>   or a something different that's not glam and that's fine 'cause I don't do
>   that all the time bitch I do ratchet hood sultry sexy or my creativity is either
>   doin some Nicki Minaj or some Cardi B you know with some colored hair
>   colored outfit you know something crazy

Foxxi also uses *sexy* and *sultry* as descriptors of her drag, terms which carry with them sexual and largely positive connotations. Since *ratchet* occurs with *hood*, directly after *glam*, however, it is hard to say whether Foxxi is using it to imply sexuality or to describe a visual aesthetic that differs from the "old school." Either way, Foxxi's comparisons of "old school" aesthetics and the styles she enjoys performing lend some insight into the privilege granted to the styles of White drag performers (i.e., traditionally country, Vegas, and Broadway/showgirl numbers) over music and performances that are indexical or celebratory of non-White music and culture.

Foxxi, an African American[2] performer who identifies openly as a trans woman and performs female-presenting drag, also mentions "doin some Nicki Minaj or some Cardi B.," referencing that she lip-syncs to the music of two well-known female rappers of color. As the comparisons of "old school drag" and newer drag rely on more personal experience and explanation from Foxxi, she demonstrates how intricately woven are her ideas about class, identity, race, and artistic ambition. All of this is evident in her depiction of the community, within this specific LGBTQ+ locale, and how that intersects with Oklahoma as a region.

Foxxi's unpacking of the "old school" label is informative and complex— she is hardly the only performer to use these words to characterize the scene— but one subtlety in her initial response in excerpt 1 cannot be overlooked: she remarks that Oklahoma drag has changed. Her authority on this subject stems from her long-held position in the community and her rise to popularity within the scene. "Old school" describes a drag performance aesthetic that was pervasive in much of the history of drag in the Gayborhood and can still be seen in some parts of the community today, while the change is the result of younger performers who in the last decade or two have begun to break away from the more traditional styles of performance.

Kelly, a Caucasian cisgender male performer of female impersonation, with nearly two decades of experience, characterizes parts of the scene as old school. She[3] remarks that 39th Street has become somewhat predictable, at least in terms of the performers who are regularly booked at venues. She alludes to the fact that drag shows in Oklahoma City were scarcer in the past and that, because of their more infrequent occurrences, felt more special ("kind of an amazing thing").

> Excerpt 3. Kelly on some changes in the Gayborhood ◀ẟ
>
> KELLY: used to um if you got to see a drag show it was uh kind of an amazing thing it was cool you know there were just a few a week now there's a show at every bar every night um I don't work a whole lot of Oklahoma City anymore just because of that fact that um I know if I want to see a certain drag queen I can go to a certain bar every night it's always the same queens in every show every single night

You would expect the rising frequency of drag shows to be celebrated by a performer. However, the latter half of Kelly's statement seems to assume a relationship between the regularity of the casts at different shows and why she works less in Oklahoma City; that is, while the number of shows has grown in the scene, Kelly suggests that this does not necessarily mean that the number of entertainers performing has increased. Her thoughts here appear, at first, to relate only to the audience's experience; there is less variety in types of entertainment, at least as far as what is regularly offered at a given venue.

Considering Kelly's position as another performer, however, highlights another important component of this scene. Her attention to the increase of popularity, frequency, and regularity of drag shows reminds us that to be a headliner, particularly one who is employed (i.e., not contracted on an event-to-event basis), is to have one of the most prestigious positions available. Not everyone in these positions is equally praised or admired by the rest of the community, but these regularly employed performers often carry some clout in the decisions made about who gets booked at various gigs and shows in their employer's venue. It is not too difficult to imagine how this can lead to problems in diversification of performances; Foxxi mentioned in one conversation that "every club has their token black girl," a rather disappointing reality for such a community.

Experienced performers have more personal history to draw upon when characterizing the drag scene in the Gayborhood, but a difference in years of experience does not stop newer performers from weighing in on the discussion, particularly regarding the availability of decently paying gigs in the scene. Guin, who identifies as a Caucasian transgender woman and has with less than a year of experience as a performer in the scene, offers her opinion of these shows and their lack of diversity.

Excerpt 4. Guin on the quality of regular shows ◀))
GUIN: you know who in their right mind wouldn't want to book someone who doesn't bring people in or don't like– or like– likes her stuff but it still happens because you're not what they– you're not– they– they wanna hold up this image but my thing is like okay it's 2019 in Oklahoma your bar hasn't changed in years your image is fading girl and it's not– it's not– it's not– you may be– your girls may be polished but your show's not polished it's boring as fuck

Guin alludes to three factors in the problem of diversifying regular bookings: the audience and their preferences; the managers/owners/senior performers who make the decisions on bookings; and by implication, the newer performers. Guin is aware of the importance of providing entertainment to the audience and its symbiotic relationship to the bar/drag shows, and she implies that the older, long-held positions in the regular shows are not necessarily bringing in crowds.

She credits the individual performers and their talents, and in a way that appears to be addressing the managers of the shows. The conditional mood ("your girls may be polished") is juxtaposed with the negated indicative ("your show's not polished") in ways that are structurally and somewhat phonetically[4] parallel, so that we are extra clear that the compliment of the individuals is not to be extended to the show and the system of bookings behind it. She punctuates this, in a way, by labeling this unnamed show "boring as fuck," echoing Kelly in excerpt 3.

Alexander, a drag king (i.e., male-presentation of drag)[5] who also had less than a year of experience performing in the Gayborhood at the time of this interview, noted the problematic lack of diversify as well. Before it closed in 2018, he and his drag peers performed primarily at the Wreck Room, a popular spot for the LGBTQ+ youth of the area, being the only 18-and-up venue for drag on "the strip." At the time of Alexander's recording session, just after the Wreck Room's closing, many younger performers and patrons openly lamented the loss of both a safe space for community youth and a site for experimental forms of drag that reflected the changing fashions and norms of the next generation.

> Excerpt 5. Alexander and Rae on lack of diversity in Oklahoma City drag ◀))
> ALEXANDER: um here lately some clubs have been called out for some stuff now I'm not gonna get too deep into that because I'm not about the drama or anything but honestly from what I see there is a lot of diversity in the ones that are getting booked but it's diversity in size really
> RAE: yeah
> ALEXANDER: I don't really see a lot of African American people like our Ravishing Rae
> RAE: [aye]
> ALEXANDER: [going out] and getting these bookings now I do see some people getting them but they're like the sticks like itty-bitty [skinny]
> RAE: [petite]
> ALEXANDER: petite yes thank you so that's just me and like I'm constantly thr– scrolling through Facebook looking you know "hey who's getting booked who do I wanna go see tonight oh it's the same people every night"
> RAE: [m-hm]
> ALEXANDER: [shit]

Alexander's sensitivity to the rising tension on the issue of diversification is revealed in his otherwise ambiguous reference to "some stuff" for which "some clubs" have been "called out." His decision not to offer more details or opinions on the matter speak to the gravity of community-straining tensions on 39th Street. There had in fact been an ongoing conversation, largely on social media outlets, confronting this problem while I was collecting data. And they still cause rifts among the various cliques and families of drag performers. Recall that Kelly and Guin offer the same critique of the scene, tethering the static casts to a lack of excitement in shows and hinting at the added difficulty for new performers to get their start in the scene.

Gizele, a self-identified Black cis-male performer with nearly a decade of experience doing female impersonation in the scene, hints at this, too, citing that Oklahoma City drag used to be even less diverse than it is today, characterizing it as "very cookie cutter" drag—a phrasing that, in light of the "old school" label, likely alludes to both the ethnoracial makeup and musical stylings of the cookie-cutter mold. Gizele does acknowledge that the few changes in casts have been good, and Foxxi claims that "if you do your research" you might see some diversity in terms of race and background compared to previous eras of the Oklahoma City drag scene, though this suggests that such diversification is not apparent.

Foxxi and Gizele's opinions as experienced performers in the scene might render them more nuanced, if not more careful, in their characterization of the scene. While everyone acknowledges the hardships faced by aspiring entertainers, the less experienced performers seem to more directly acknowledge this.

Describing Drag and the Scene: "Cutthroat." When asked how he would describe drag in Oklahoma, Alexander does not focus on the stylings of dress, makeup, or music in his response. Unlike Foxxi, who was able to account for a history of the area, Alexander seems to focus entirely on his experience, along with Rae, his drag sister (a member of his familial community within broader community of practice). Rae self-identifies as Black/AA and transgender and performs in self-described "feminine" and "female" presentation.

In except 6, Rae echoes Alexander's description, but distinguishes Oklahoma City from bigger cities with well-known drag scenes. Alexander continues the list of big cities, but he quickly acknowledges "a reason" for the "cutthroat" nature, tying it to the small numbers in Oklahoma City and the relative amplification of celebrity status in the community.

> Excerpt 6. Alexander and Rae on the "cutthroat" Oklahoma City drag scene ◄))
> INTERVIEWER: how would you describe what drag is like in Oklahoma
> ALEXANDER: cutthroat [((sucks teeth))]
> RAE: [yeah] cut[throat]
> ALEXANDER: [um]
> RAE: but– but not as cutthroat as Las Vegas Texas
> ALEXANDER: New York California

RAE: true

ALEXANDER: it's cut throat yeah but it's cut throat for a reason there's so few of us here that the the the ones that do get booked are the ones that are like top dog as a lot of people would say

RAE: m-hm

ALEXANDER: uh but the ones that don't get booked we're trying to get that booking we're trying to make a name for ourselves

RAE: it is [hard]

ALEXANDER: [so we've] got to battle those ones that are always booked so

Thus, for the newer performers, they must "battle" the established performers for stage time, a war metaphor whose nuance can be found in the other discussions and descriptions of the power dynamics within this community. While the newer performers appear to demonstrate a more direct characterization of Oklahoma City's drag community as cutthroat, they are not alone in pointing out this tendency of the scene, nor even to use that exact descriptor. Below in excerpt 7, Kelly describes some of the experiences she has had as a long-time performer in the scene; that same excerpt offers (separate interviews) Foxxi's comments on competition in the scene. In both cases, the term *cutthroat* is employed.

Excerpt 7. Kelly on her experience; Foxxi on competition; "cutthroat" ◀))

KELLY: uh for one you have to have thick skin because it is cutthroat like I said y– you know competition with ((inhales)) more established queens they can be really cutthroat um

INTERVIEWER: how so

KELLY: ((sucks teeth)) it's really hard to get into the shows like for myself um for my first 13 years of drag um I was in any show that I wanted to be in Oklahoma City then I quit drag for two years [...] and when I came back the entire scene had changed and people who were my friends that I worked with all the time had moved on to other bars or had finally gotten their own shows um and they would not book me

[...]

FOXXI: it's so cutthroat eith– 'cause like either they feel competition so they wanna like either try to bring you down break you down to make you feel inferior or unconfident but that– they doin that because they know that you're competition

Kelly first uses the term *cutthroat* as a reason for needing "thick skin" in this community, something she mentions elsewhere as it relates to throwing shade, that is, exchanging ritual insults that tend to focus on drag appearance and performance. Throwing shade appears to have its roots in African American language and culture as well, looking much like the dozens, which Smitherman (1994, 100) characterizes as being used "to test not only [play-

ers'] verbal skills but also their capacity to maintain their COOL." In excerpt 7,
Kelly references competition with other queens, offering personal experience
of her own that presumably demonstrates the types of cutthroat or competitive
behaviors in the community. She mentions her absence from the scene,[6] a
short two years compared to her then 13-year record in the community but
a great deal of time in terms of the opportunities for change in this community. This absence appears to have cost her the freedom of performing
"in any show that [she] wanted," now positioning herself as competition
with performers who "were" her friends. This competitive coloring of the
community is consistent across every participant in this study, though they
vary in how and in what contexts they do so.

Foxxi uses the term *cutthroat* to refer to the competitive nature of critique,
shade, and the arguments various performers get into (online and in person).
She describes the surface motivation for such criticisms as seeking to make
someone feel "unconfident" or to "break [them] down," but offers a nuanced
understanding of them as well: "they doin that because they know that you
competition." For both Kelly and Foxxi, the cutthroat nature of the scene is
tied to the competitive situation that almost all performers find themselves
in. It is at least implied that Kelly lost friends over this sort of phenomenon,
while Foxxi explains, perhaps normalizes, and certainly contextualizes the
types of language-related "cutthroat" behavior that occurs in the scene.

These insights have led to a better understanding of the overall
characterization of Oklahoma City drag, particularly as it pertains to the long-
held privileged status of White, broadway- and Vegas-inspired performances
and the work it takes to be successful (or simply to earn money) in the scene.
Still, these insights in the "old school" and "cutthroat" tendencies of the scene
do not capture the diversity in audiences or in up-and-coming talent, nor
do these depictions adequately convey the relative seclusion of 39th Street
from the rest of Oklahoma City or how that seclusion bolsters the community
roles in complicated and important ways.

THE 39TH STREET VENUES. The six major sites for this investigation were
The Boom, Tramps, Phoenix Rising, The Copa Cabana, The Finishline,
and the Wreck Room. The discourse presented here details the state of the
Gayborhood at the time of recording, which is depicted with labels of these
and other relevant sites in figure 1.

Participants of this project were all asked about whether there were
different audiences at different venues, and almost everyone had something
different to say. Their responses, like those characterizing Oklahoma drag,
revolved around their own drag experience. Almost all participants associated
certain venues with certain milestones of their journeys as performers. That
is, venues are referenced in these data according to the type of drag found

FIGURE 1
The Oklahoma City "Gayborhood"

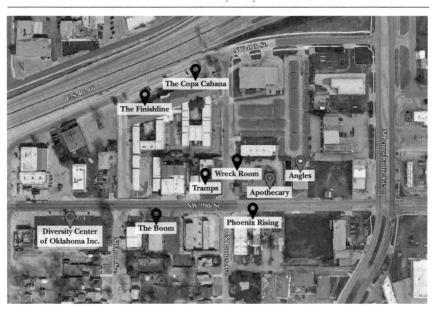

in them, but also according to the status afforded by performing at certain venues.

Excerpt 8. Alexander and Rae on some of the different venues ◀)

RAE: Sunday nights here at Tramps the place is packed barely for a place to sit and that's–

ALEXANDER: you've got the people here for the classic drag here

RAE: yeah

ALEXANDER: at Tramps and then The Boom you go there and it's the younger community

RAE: uh-huh

ALEXANDER: they wanna see the ratchet they wanna see the upbeat

RAE: ♪that ass, that ass, that [ass]♪

ALEXANDER: [I mean]

[...]

ALEXANDER: The Boom is the younger generation of

RAE: [well]

ALEXANDER: [I'm] just gonna say it's the younger gays the Phoenix [it's the old]

RAE: [((exhales))]

ALEXANDER: rich gays like this is how we decide whether or not we're going to a show "do you wanna join me tonight" "where's it at" "Phoenix" "old rich gays I'm going"

RAE: yeah

ALEXANDER: "do you wanna join me tonight" "where's it at" "Wreck Room"
RAE: [and]
ALEXANDER: "[kids] nah I'm good"

Rae and Alexander, for example, immediately discuss Tramps—the venue where this particular segment of the recording took place—by mentioning popularity ("place is packed")[7] and the aesthetic ("classic drag"), the latter of which is probably tied to the oft-termed "old school drag." They then discuss The Boom, where we are told about the typical audience ("the younger community")[8] and the aesthetic ("the ratchet [...] upbeat," "that ass, that ass").[9] This conversation then seems to pick up in the comparative work by Alexander, who then juxtaposes The Boom ("younger gays") with the Rising Phoenix ("old rich gays"), factors that presumably play a role in his decision where to spend his evening.

The follow-up to this includes another performative exchange in which Alexander notes the Wreck Room is where the "kids"[10] are at. As the Wreck Room is a venue that allows patrons age 18 and older to enter, we see an important distinction between the "young community," made up of young adult patrons old enough to purchase liquor, and the "kid kids," who cannot.[11] This characterization of the Wreck Room is constant throughout every interview and group discussion: it is an old venue associated with underage audiences and aspiring young performers. Copa gets labeled "the weird,"[12] which Alexander associates with some of the other, less-popularized subcultures of queer communities (e.g., leather, kink, role-playing; see Barrett 2017)—in this instance, this *weird* does not necessarily carry with it overtly negative or evaluative connotations.

Many young LGBTQ+ Oklahomans throughout the years have made their way to the Wreck Room at some point. A safe space for queer and trans youth, and it was, for many, the first step in making a name for oneself on the drag scene. In one group discussion, Foxxi, who has been rather successful,[13] shared the following story of the first drag show she ever went to.[14]

Excerpt 9. Foxxi on the first drag show she ever saw ◀))
FOXXI: when I went to my first drag show and if– and you know what I'm saying like just being a gay boy you feel liberated you feel good you feel like– you feel accepted like "oh my god I love what they're doing it's a good time" um I didn't– like my first drag show I like– on the sideline I was dancing my ass off 'cause I loved the mus– music they were doing you know I just felt just havin fun I wasn't tryna showboat I just was myself you know I'm just dancing bitch just getting my life ((clap)) and I wasn't tryin to like necessarily steal the show but it was a Wreck Room show and I– like was just having fun it was my first time being out as a gay dude you just a gay per– you know just a gay dude like this my first time like I've never been to a gay club I'm just

living my life and you know me I love to dance so bitch they playin all the good music well attention got kinda like shown over to me at the very end of the show the club was over and then one of the queens like literally came outside as we was leaving and ran up and was like "I love what you were doing but you know the show's not about you so don't try to take over" you know I was like ((shocked face)) and my best friend she was like "well he wants to be a drag queen" and she was like "everybody wants to be a drag queen" and walked off

Foxxi's story offers more nuance than there is space to cover, but it appears to be marked both by the freedom found in a safe space to be queer and by the competitive tension created in such safe spaces among the various entertainers of the crowds.

More specifically, this unnamed drag queen[15] appears to be potentially threatened by the attention Foxxi got just by dancing, and she does not seem to think much of young Foxxi's desire to partake in drag culture and entertainment. This has proven to be a commonality across this study: established performers (regardless of levels of experience) acknowledge the ever-growing popularity of drag and the oversimplified perception of what it takes to do drag. The work it takes to make a name in this community helps to explain the defensive position many performers take when hearing of a new person who wants to pick up drag as though it were a weekend hobby.

A final point emerges from this excerpt: that such competitive spirits roam even in the Wreck Room, where so many young queer people see their first drag show, and where so many young aspiring performers get their first gig. Foxxi's account of this story was introduced as the first time she ever saw a drag show; as an established performer herself, it is no wonder she sees this as a part of her journey and emphasizes the role of the confrontation in the story.

The Wreck Room's unique position among the other venues has other affects as well. While most of the other venues have more regular shows with more regular casts, the young and revolving cast at the Wreck Room demanded new, innovative, boundary-pushing performances that challenged the norms of the community.[16] For this reason, Kelly, who has more years of experience than any other performer in this study, claimed "I have to prove myself more in Wreck Room than I have to at any other place" when she hosted there. Alexander and Rae said that, despite the differences in crowds and venues, the Wreck Room was their favorite because of the openness of what counted as drag, what got booked, and how the crowd reacted to.

One other venue has played a role in the changing tides of Oklahoma City drag. The Boom is deserving of some specific attention because of the college-aged crowd it attracts, because of the status offered by performing at this venue, and because the occasional diversity of its cast. Still, there are some aspects to The Boom that rely on more traditional, if not conservative, approaches to drag. Gizele comments that it is still influenced by a classic sort of Vegas-style of show.

> Excerpt 10. Gizele on drag at The Boom
> INTERVIEWER: are there differences in audiences or venues
> GIZELE: most definitely like The Boom is very much a show bar and it's very kinda Vegas style so you're not just gonna get a drag show you're also gonna get kind of that experience […] you wouldn't see Foxxi at The Boom back in the day
> FOXXI: hell naw bitch

Vegas showgirls are said to be one of the proposed early influences on drag culture (see Newton 1979), while Harlem ball culture has been identified as a more direct influence on the drag culture of today (see *Paris Is Burning* 1990). These are important historical points to keep in mind for their different potential inspirations in today's drag scene, and they are worth extra critical attention given that the former was an entertainment industry dominated by cisgender White female performers and the latter by a collective and expressive cultural celebration practiced by predominantly queer and trans working-class Black and Latinx people in New York City. In excerpt 10, Gizele makes a further point by saying that Foxxi would not have been seen working there in the past (though she boasted a regular headliner position there at the time of Gizele's saying this), presumably a comment on both the requirements to work at The Boom and the credentials a younger Foxxi might not have had. Foxxi, who was present in the group discussion, immediately agrees, and elsewhere, she elaborates that she has grown as a performer and that she has learned to appreciate some of the pageantry.

In many ways, because Foxxi is a headliner at The Boom, she offers a perspective not available to many of the other performers in this study. Recalling that the crowd is predominantly younger, college-aged people who are (to put it frankly) more interested in today's popular music than they are classic, Broadway, or showgirl musicals, it is no wonder that Foxxi explicitly states "I have to put the crowd out before I do anything. I know what they wanna hear." That is, Foxxi's discussion of The Boom centers around her role there at the time of the interview, as an employed, regularly performing entertainer for large audiences, a substantial portion of which are serious fans of hers. On the nights that I spent observing and talking with Foxxi while she was performing or hosting a show at The Boom, every small conversation between sets was interrupted by new and old fans expressing their adoration of her. As she walks through a crowd to get a drink before her next number, she is constantly hugged, kissed, touched, hollered at, and offered drinks. And when she does get on stage for her number, the room almost always explodes with cheers and applause. It's no wonder that here at The Boom, the location of our first recorded interview and a place that helped her grow her celebrity, she thinks of the crowd.

Foxxi also mentions the other venues, like the Rising Phoenix, which she describes as "more burlesque" in its shows, citing that there was a little deviation from the Vegas-type classic drag, but she holds there is more variety in the regular performances at The Boom. This description is accompanied by Foxxi's story of her earlier career in drag and the Phoenix's first trial at hosting drag performances. She notes that the managers of the venue were very particular about the type of drag they wanted in their shows. She has since performed many times at the Phoenix, and her memories of these early days appear to encourage her ability to be uniquely herself while having to adhere to some of the norms of the community.

Foxxi's talk about her early days at the Rising Phoenix centers around the managers' prioritization of making money. The view of drag as a money-making enterprise is certainly not new; Esther Newton's *Mother Camp* (1979) references the early drag industry in Vegas, the economic role it played there, and the work ethic it took for early performers "on the job." Today, however, the commodification of drag via popular media and television appears to make the economics of drag as prevalent as the creative and expressive components to the performance.

As a reminder, all respondents tend to describe venues as they correspond to their own experiences or memories at certain shows of these venues. Kelly, for example, mentions that she does not work in Oklahoma City much anymore, citing the changed scene and "cutthroat" nature of some seasoned queens as her reason. She says that she does not mind going to The Boom, of all places, to work "for free"[17] on Thursday nights. These nights are typically for newer and less-popular talent who lack regular bookings on more popular nights of the week, thus the performers are paid less.

Kelly, in the unique position of performing for little money at The Boom and often hosting the younger performers at the Wreck Room before its closing, describes herself as apparently "old school" to the younger performers, while she is seen as "new school" to the older and long-established performers. Moreover, Kelly has a career outside of drag—not altogether uncommon, but most performers' other jobs are in the service industry, while Kelly's is in the medical field. Her financial stability means that she can go to such events without worry that she will be wasting her time (i.e., working without earning), whereas other performers who have more need for the income are likely to pursue more lucrative opportunities.

Even the brief focus on the two venues given most attention here (Wreck Room and The Boom) demonstrates both overlap and distinction among the responses to the economics of the practice, to the influence of age and popular culture, and to the seemingly ever-present lines of division across race, class, and styles of drag. In many ways, The Boom is always the most popularly mentioned venue, and certainly more prestigious than the Wreck Room. However, the audience at The Boom is far more critical of the performers than the Wreck Room—a fact cited by Kelly, Gizele, and Foxxi, who all have or do perform there. Much in the way that the characterization of the scene overall is influenced by experience and perspective, the general conversations about these venues revolve around the way that speakers see it: Wreck Room is the (kid) kids place and/or the safe space; The Boom is the hippest and/or the toughest place. This experience appears to intersect with roles in the community, where we see shifts between aspiring performer and established talent affecting the ways certain venues are described. This is also affected by identity work in distinguishing between seasoned performer and/or newcomer or perhaps hustler (i.e., someone who is working nonstop to be successful in their drag endeavors).

The added pressure of entertainment is something threaded throughout the discussions, something that fuels the competition and tension among performers but also fosters a need for community and family, especially for so many young queer Oklahomans who have been estranged or are otherwise never accepted by their biological families, especially parents and guardians, for who they are. For this reason, the final section of the analysis discusses the importance of queer and drag kinship in this community.

COMMUNITY: QUEER KINSHIP SYSTEMS
IN OKLAHOMA CITY DRAG

No study on drag performance, whether language specific or otherwise, could be conducted without considering drag culture, and drag family is one of the most important and pervasive components of drag culture. Put most directly, drag family encompasses a complex queer kinship system (see below) that spans across various types of relationships, almost all of which have corresponding familial labels (e.g., *mother, father, son, cousin, aunt,* etc.). There is a sense in which this system is adequately captured by Sahlins's (2013) "mutuality of being," which may offer "the virtue of describing the various means by which kinship may be constituted, whether natally or postnatally, from pure 'biology' to pure performance, and any combinations thereof" (28). This formulation of "being" thus extends beyond traditional views of shared DNA, or even for the case of Oklahoma City's drag community, shared ancestral or ethnoracial heritage. Indeed Sahlins proposes that procreation and performance are but alternate forms of kinship, arguing that kinship at its heart is in fact cultural and not biological.

Some of the kinship roles played by community members, in and out of "drag families" (whose drag personae often donn a family or house "last name"), appear to be products of African American cultural influence, most notably "play cousins" and other "play family" (see Green 2019; Simmons-Horton et al. 2022). And while there has been work that addresses kinship in relation to discussions of drag—almost entirely concerning RuPaul's TV franchises (e.g., LeMaster 2015; Shetina 2018)—even these depictions of queer kinship seem to approach what Walters (2012) warns of in popular depictions of queer kinship: pushing queer kinship toward normative models of what "family" constitutes. While biological kinship terms are often employed in Oklahoma City's drag family units—and there are certainly performative overlaps across different kinfolk roles—the local drag circuit provides unique, complex, and nuanced components to the roles that are otherwise lost in a broader models of queer-as-kinship, specifically when it comes to the competitive nature of booking drag gigs.

This particular web of social connections within drag-performing communities has been documented before (e.g., *Paris Is Burning* 1991). The world which working-class Black and Latinx people of color in 1980s Harlem drag culture was built around performance and kinship. Competition plays a role, too, but kinship has been both an integral aspect of drag culture and an often necessary resource for queer and trans people (see Eng 2010), particularly in places like Oklahoma, who find themselves suddenly without family or support for expressing their noncisgender identities and/or non-heterosexual identities or orientations.

Drag family, then, is much more important than simple familial labels. In most cases, the labels indicate a relational role between one person and another of their family unit. For example, Foxxi is both a drag mother and a drag daughter.[18] In an interview about doing her first drag show, she recalls the very first time she met her drag mother-to-be. When she saw her would-be drag mother and drag aunt in the dressing room behind a stage, they were the first African American drag queens she had ever seen in Oklahoma City. Foxxi notes that she fell in love with her drag mother because she, like Foxxi, has a bigger frame and is not a petite performer ("she's thick like me"). She offers some of her internal thought process by performing quotative material—an interpretation encouraged by the frequent employment of quotative *like*.

Foxxi tells that, despite her admiration for her drag mother, she felt she had to win a pageant title before officially asking to be her daughter. Foxxi's drag mother, in fact, was already a successful, well-known, club-performing, and pageant-winning drag queen by the time they met. Foxxi's desire to establish herself is indicative of the respect shown successful performers—perhaps especially performers of color who manage to achieve success even with the ideologies affecting bookings and audiences. The unnamed drag queen who told Foxxi, "Everybody wants to be a drag queen" (excerpt 9), helps us understand that there is some uphill work to be done to earn the respect, or at least professional acknowledgment, of other performers. Still, Foxxi gives herself a little credit by noting that her drag mother, upon finally being asked to be her mentor, only replied, "I've been waiting."

Drag mothers may very well nurture and care for their drag children, but they also function professionally as a mentor beyond appearances and dress, helping newer performers get bookings, meet other well-known performers, and spend time in the scene's inner circles. This is not to downplay the importance of a drag mother's role in helping craft a particular style or aesthetic. These are crucial parts of drag culture. Kelly hints at this, stating if someone gets a gig at The Boom, "You really need someone to be able to guide you" or run the risk of being "torn apart" by the audience/other performers.

Guin, Foxxi's drag daughter, also offered insights on the importance of drag mentorship. She notes below that Oklahoma is small and that the drag scene (in terms of sheer numbers) is perhaps small, but despite its relative isolation, it has managed to attract considerable attention from nearby states. She notes that it is easy to find a drag mother but with a caveat.

Excerpt 11. Guin on drag mothers in Oklahoma ◄))
GUIN: and I feel like because Oklahoma is small like it is a small place but we are– we're so known everyone is– really wants to hold that title and they are afraid of anybody taking it so because of that they are very– it's easy to find a drag mother[19] here yes and find someone to help you if you're wanting that help ((inhales)) better make sure you get a damn good drag mom 'n' drag family 'cause if not you are gonna be torn to shreds […] drag queens are very open and accepting and diverse but we also do not welcome that very much either

Guin's warning that one should "make sure you get a damn good drag mom and drag family" has at least two important points to it. Drag family can help learn the tricks of the trade, help with appearance and performance, and hopefully help anticipate the types of acts to be performed at certain events. The second might be more crucial for success: networking. It is imperative for drag performers to build a network as best they can with other performers, inside and outside of their families, in order to be considered for various non-recurring events.[20] Without such mentorship, one might be "torn to shreds."

It is of no surprise that Guin mentions this thought, being the drag daughter of Foxxi, a well-known performer who is the drag daughter of another well-known performer. In many ways, Guin must carry both the burden of being her drag mother's daughter (expected to be good enough to warrant the relationship) without appearing to copy her drag mother too much. But she also inherits the privilege of being better known than many other performers with her level of experience who do not have drag family with such status.

Guin also notes that, because Oklahoma is so small but so successful in its thriving drag culture, it can cause difficulties for some community-internal relationships and events. This sheds light on the fact that Oklahoma City, admittedly one of the more RELATIVELY progressive places in Oklahoma,[21] has a history of conservative political and sociocultural thought and behavior. The Gayborhood had a its own history of fending off police brutality and discrimination. Because of that fight, much of this area has grown as a separate part of the city. In many ways, because of the tenuous situation so many young LGBTQ+ people face, this safe zone provides a place to build queer kinship when they are denied access to traditional kinship outside of this community. These relationships among drag community members are bolstered by the queer communities' strength in its centralized locale and the separation of that locale from Oklahoma City as a whole. As drag performers are local celebrities, especially successful and regularly performing ones, they are given a lot of attention and admiration in this community. These kinship relationships are at least potentially magnified in their importance because of the role the performers play in the community.

The complexities that exist between the "outside" world beyond the Gayborhood and the community-internal relationships manifest in some of the discourse on drag family in more direct ways than Foxxi or Guin have exampled. Alexander and Rae share a drag father. When asked about the cost of drag, they discussed the importance of asking for help, something they learned from their drag father.

Excerpt 12. Alexander and Rae on drag family and helping out ◀))

INTERVIEWER: is this something that you think the whole community takes part in borrowing and like asking for help

RAE: no

ALEXANDER: no [uh]

RAE: [people] most performers let their pride and the ego get in the way of asking for help or asking for anything in general but like dad said "ask ask ask ask"

ALEXANDER: if you don't ask you'll never know

RAE: [yeah]
ALEXANDER: [um] for instance [drag dad] borrowed couple of my costumes last
        night and he went up to Norman now granted I didn't get to debut them in
        Norman but that's fine cause they got to be seen in Norman um I'm going
        to hopefully go to Tulsa next Thursday if my ankle's healed and perform
        there and debut some costumes there um but if you don't ask how to make
        something or if you can borrow something or how to do something you're
        never gonna know
RAE: yeah true
[...]
ALEXANDER: I know myself I have been in positions where like right now me
        and my wife we're technically homeless 'cause we got kicked out of my
        [biological] mom's thank god for my [drag] sisters they let us move in um
        I feel like I owe a lot of people a great debt for helping me get to where I
        am today I really do and I tell them this every *time* and I don't think people
        quite understand that I don't accept help unless I have a way to pay them
        back ((inhales)) and I do thank you Celeste and Rae, for helping us out
        and *doing all this for me.*
RAE: uh-uh don't you [start doin that].
ALEXANDER: [I'm trying not] to cry
RAE: do not start cry– I will backhand you back to Bangkok don't you do it

Alexander mentions his drag father has recently borrowed some of his
new drag outfits and took them to an event to debut. Alex's comment "but
it's fine cause they got to be seen in Norman" is introduced with a contrastive
conjunction *but*, implying that there is at least a possibility that Alex could be
bothered by his father's debuting of Alexander's own new outfits before he
himself is able to. Alex ends his turn by noting that, if an aspiring performer
does not ask for help or information, "you're never gonna know."

Rae and Alexander were asked if their approach to asking for help was
influenced solely because of their drag father's teachings or because of the
situations they found themselves in. While the question was intended to
prompt discussioin of drag performance, appearance, and sartorial help,
Alexander quickly recognizes a different sort of situation for himself. Earlier
in this discussion, Alexander had described the way drag—specifically drag
at the Wreck Room—helped him discover his trans identity, find the community who would support him in his transitioning, and find the courage to
take the journey of becoming more authentically himself. This was a source
of conflict with his biological mother, who eventually cut ties with Alexander
over it. Alexander's drag sisters, Celeste and Rae, had opened up their place
for him and his wife to stay in the meantime. Alexander's voice breaks in
expressing his gratitude, indicated with italic.

In response to Alexander's emotional statement of gratitude, Rae tells him that he better not cry, which brings laughter around the whole group. Rae's diversion from the thanks offered toward her and Celeste, however, also alludes to the complexity of the drag kinship system in its relationship to the world "outside." That is, this type of togetherness, of loyalty and dependability for family who need help, is reflective of the ideal traditional kinship system outside the community, yet it is also reflective of the fact that many queer and trans Oklahomans are denied access to such systems. More aptly, Rae is aware that this is just what you are supposed to do for your family. It is especially necessary among queer relationships because of their necessity in finding shelter, safety, and support in being true to oneself.

CONCLUSIONS: LAYERS AND LAYERS

This article has attempted to use observational, discursive, and sociolinguistic data to describe parts of Oklahoma City's 39th Street District and the thriving drag performance community within it. Every step taken, however, to study a piece of it (e.g., the region of Oklahoma, the smaller region of Oklahoma City, the place of 39th Street, the LGBTQ+ community there, the drag community of practice, etc.) reveals that no one depiction, no matter how small or particular, captures the layered, intersectional, and historically rich site that is the Oklahoma City drag circuit. Rather, this study has focused on the explicit and implicational relaying of what it has been like to be a drag performer in this scene, and the language shows that it is not the same for everyone.

By addressing the ever-present phantom of "old school" types of drag, which is said to characterize most of the traditional venues, the respondents directly and indirectly relay the privilege afforded White, often cisgender, Vegas- and Broadway-inspired modes of performance. This has also contributed to the competitive, "cutthroat" nature of the area, indicating that making a name for oneself, getting booked, and finding success in the scene is not always about talent and aspiration. While these thematic foci were critical to the groundwork of ethnography and community complexity, it should also be noted that the language component is equally as influential. Performers employ drag-related language and stylistics, much of which has been influenced by AAL varieties, and they reference local phenomena in ways that hint at the regularity with which these features are used—something any dialectological study of Oklahoma, or even Oklahoma City, would no doubt find difficult documenting.

The discourse produced by newer performers complicated the characterization of the Gayborhood, offering perspectives that are necessarily different from established and employed performers. This difference is somehow magnified with the discussions of the Wreck Room, knowing that it is now closed, and reveals that the role of drag kinship systems is evermore necessary in the successful development and maintenance of a presence in the drag in Oklahoma City. Drag family, then, is revealed to be a critical part of the drag community in Oklahoma City, a fact bolstered in importance by the role drag plays in the wider LGBTQ+ community and in the role kinship plays in providing shelter and family to queer youth who are otherwise without such support. Finally, this necessitates a rethinking of how sociolinguists talk about region, about place, and about community. For this study, at least, the analysis of discursive identity construction is necessary to understand the intersectional complexity of the place. And to gloss over any of those complexities is to undoubtedly miss some of the most meaningful and insightful aspects of what place can be.

NOTES

I would like to especially thank Courtney Bandy, who has been a friend, a teacher, and an invaluable asset in helping introduce me to this community and conduct this research. I would also like to thank the participants, the persevering and inspiring drag performers and community members who are too often facing pushback for the celebration of LGBTQ+ existence. Last but not least, I would like to thank Dennis Preston, my mentor and friend, for always providing indispensable advice and for always being there.

1. Transcriptions do not account for intonation units or pauses. Three periods represent elided content. To focus on the speech of the participants, backchannels, laughter, and nonlinguistic noises from the interviewer or others present are not included unless deemed relevant to the analysis, though they are audible in the accompanying audio clips embedded in the online PDFs of this article (https://doi.org/10.1215/00031283-10579442). Note, embedded media are not supported by all PDF viewers; if you are unable to access it using your viewer, try opening the PDF in Adobe's free Acrobat Reader, http://get.adobe.com/reader/.

2. Labels for ethnicity, gender, and other identity categories are taken from the demographic information sheet filled out by respondents in their own words and are here used as a best attempt to represent their original words. While I acknowledge that it is not always necessary to include demographic labels for race and gender, I include them here because of their relevance to the community and the sociocultural and sociolinguistic complexities within it.

3. The tradition of referencing performers pronominally defaults to the gender they present in drag, despite gender identity outside of drag performance; most performers still use these pronouns outside of drag as well.

4. The two clauses are somewhat phonetically parallel in that *girls* has a voiced plural morpheme [-z] and *show's* has a contracted copula [-z]

5. Alexander openly identifies as a While male and talks of his being assigned female at birth and how drag led to his realization that he is a trans man; see note 9.

6. Kelly discloses in the interview that, following a bad car accident, she had to take time to physically recover from her injuries, more still before she was strong enough to perform on stage again (in heels).

7. It should be noted that this popularity or big crowd is constrained by the particular day. Not many would have shown up to Copa on a Sunday, but Tramps could still be packed. However, if it were a Thursday and The Boom were packed, you would probably get spill-over into Tramps.

8. The "younger community" here should be disambiguated from the underage crowd at Wreck Room; rather, they are college-aged.

9. Here, interestingly where Foxxi performs, Alexander uses the term *ratchet* to describe the aesthetic. Alexander's use of AAL-related lexical items speaks of their popularity in broader drag culture, certainly within this community, and of shared linguistic traits among drag family groups (more in the next section)

10. Notice also the use of duplicative "kid kids" to designate younger-than the "younger community."

11. It is a sort of unsaid truth that some of these youth who find a way in are, in fact, not even 18.

12. The nominal adjective *the weird* occurs frequently in this data set.

13. Foxxi has been a regularly booked performer, one of the few African American performers to be consistently so; and she has won a number of local and regional drag pageants.

14. When Foxxi offered this reflection (excerpt 9), she had already shared that her experience with drag led to her coming out as trans; however, because this experience occurred before that realization, Foxxi's use of pronouns reflects how she was referenced before coming out. These pronouns are, for the purposes of honoring the data and the perspective offered by Foxxi, written sic erat dictum.

15. Foxxi alluded to me who this performer was, a White drag queen who favored the "old school" drag, though she asked that all other descriptions of them be left out as they are good friends today.

16. Prior to its closing, you would be unlikely to find anything that could appropriately be called "old school drag" in this venue, perhaps with the exception of the host, who is usually a better-known performer.

17. For a seasoned performer, getting paid $10–15 for a gig is practically doing it for free.

18. In most speech, I have found that most kinship terms do not need modifying with *drag* among community members, though *drag mother* occurs more frequently

than any of the others; for the sake of consistency, *drag* will be used to modify all subsequent instances of community kinship relationships and roles.

19. I offer the clarification that Guin probably means it's easy to find any ol' drag mother.

20. These are probably the most common precursor to getting regularly booked at venues.

21. I encourage you to read this sentence with a grain of salt as Oklahoma City is still not a leader in progressive and inclusive politics, especially when it comes to LGBTQ+ populations and people of color.

REFERENCES

Associated Press. 2022. "Native American Elders Recall Abuse at US Government Boarding Schools." *The Guardian*, July 9, 2022. https://www.theguardian.com/us-news/2022/jul/09/native-american-elders-us-government-schools-oklahoma.

Bachhofer, Aaron Lee, II. 2006. "The Emergence and Evolution of the Gay and Bisexual Male Subculture in Oklahoma City, Oklahoma, 1889–2005." Ph.D. diss., Oklahoma State Univeristy.

Bailey, Guy, Jan Tillery, and Tom Wikle. 1997. "Methodology of a Survey of Oklahoma Dialects." *SECOL Review* 2, no. 1: 1–30.

Bailey, Guy, Tom Wikle, Jan Tillery, and Lori Sand. 1993. "Some Patterns of Linguistic Diffusion." *Language Variation and Change* 5, no. 3 (Oct.): 359–90. https://doi.org/10.1017/S095439450000154X.

Bakos, Jon. 2013. "A Comparison of the Speech Patterns and Dialect Attitudes of Oklahoma." Ph.D. diss., Oklahoma State Univeristy.

Barrett, Rusty. 1999. "Indexing Polyphonous Identity in the Speech of African American Drag Queens." In *Reinventing Identities: The Gendered Self in Discourse*, edited by Mary Bucholtz, A. C. Liang, and Laurel A. Sutton, 313–30. New York: Oxford University Press.

Barrett, Rusty. 2017. *From Drag Queens to Leathermen: Language, Gender, and Gay Male Subcultures*. New York: Oxford University Press.

Bucholtz, Mary. 2018. "White Affects and Sociolinguistic Activism." *Language in Society* 47, no. 3 (June): 350–54. https://doi.org/10.1017/S0047404518000271.

Bucholtz, Mary, and Kira Hall. 2005. "Identity and Interaction: A Sociocultural Linguistic Approach." *Discourse Studies* 7, nos. 4–5 (Oct.): 585–614. https://doi.org/10.1177/1461445605054407.

Bucholtz, Mary, and Kira Hall. 2008. "All of the Above: New Coalitions in Sociocultural Linguistics." In "Socio-cultural Linguistics," edited by Mary Bucholtz and Kira Hall. Special issue, *Journal of Sociolinguistics* 12, no. 4 (Sept.): 401–31. https://doi.org/10.1111/j.1467-9841.2008.00382.x.

Carbado, Devon W., Kimberlé Williams Crenshaw, Vickie M. Mays, and Barbara Tomlinson. 2013. "Intersectionality: Mapping the Movements of a Theory." *Du Bois Review: Social Science Research on Race* 10, no. 2: 303–12. https://doi.org/10.1017/S1742058X13000349.

Chang, David A. 2010. *The Color of the Land: Race, Nation, and the Politics of Landowner-ship in Oklahoma, 1832–1929.* Chapel Hill: University of North Carolina Press. https://doi.org/10.5149/9780807895764_chang.

Charity Hudley, Anne H. 2017. "Language and Racialization." In *The Oxford Handbook of Language and Society,* edited by Ofelia García, Nelson Flores, and Massimiliano Spotti, 381–402. Oxford: Oxford University Press.

Copland, Fiona, and Angela Creese. 2015. *Linguistic Ethnography: Collecting, Analysing and Presenting Data.* With Frances Rock and Sara Shaw. London: Sage.

Crenshaw, Kimberlé. 2016. "The Urgency of Intersectionality." Talk presented at TEDWomen 2016, San Francisco, Calf., Oct. 27, 2016. Available at https://www.ted.com/talks/kimberle_crenshaw_the_urgency_of_intersectionality.

Eng, David L. 2010. *The Feeling of Kinship: Queer Liberalism and the Racialization of Intimacy.* Durham, N.C.: Duke University Press.

Flores, Nelson, Mark C. Lewis, and Jennifer Phuong. 2018. "Raciolinguistic Chronotopes and the Education of Latinx Students: Resistance and Anxiety in a Bilingual School." *Language and Communication* 62, part A: 15–25. https://doi.org/10.1016/j.langcom.2018.06.002.

Green, Kai M. 2019. "In the Life: On Black Queer Kinship." *Women, Gender, and Families of Color* 7, no. 1 (Spring): 98–101. https://doi.org/10.5406/womgenfamcol.7.1.0098.

Hall-Lew, Lauren, and Nola Stephens. 2012. "Country Talk." *Journal of English Linguistics* 40, no. 3 (Sept. 2012): 256–80. https://doi.org/10.1177/0075424211420568.

Jones, Lucy. 2022. "'I'm a Boy, Can't You See That?' Dialogic Embodiment and the Construction of Agency in Trans Youth Discourse." *Language in Society.* Published ahead of print, Sept. 5, 2022. https://doi.org/10.1017/S0047404522000252.

Jones, Taylor. 2015. "Toward a Description of African American Vernacular English Dialect Regions Using 'Black Twitter.'" *American Speech,* 90, no. 4 (Nov.): 403–40. https://doi.org/10.1215/00031283-3442117.

Kvam, Dani S. 2017. "Supporting Mexican Immigrants' Resettlement in the United States: An Ethnography of Communication Approach to Building Allies' Communication Competence." *Journal of Applied Communication Research* 45, no. 1: 1–20. https://doi.org/10.1080/00909882.2016.1248469.

Labov, William, Sharon Ash, and Charles Boberg. 2006. *The Atlas of North American English: Phonetics, Phonology, and Sound Change.* Berlin: Mouton de Gruyter.

LeMaster, Benny. 2015. "Discontents of Being and Becoming Fabulous on *RuPaul's Drag U*: Queer Criticism in Neoliberal Times." *Women's Studies in Communication* 38, no. 2: 167–86. https://doi.org/10.1080/07491409.2014.988776.

Luckerson, Victor. 2021. "The Promise of Oklahoma: How the Push for Statehood Led a Beacon of Racial Progress to Oppression and Violence." *Smithsonian Magazine,* Apr. 2021. https://www.smithsonianmag.com/history/unrealized-promise-oklahoma-180977174/.

McCleary, Bryce E. 2016. "Between a Rock and a Hard Place: Investigating Gay Men, Oklahoma Dialectology, and Language Ideology." M.A. thesis, Oklahoma State Univeristy. https://hdl.handle.net/11244/300382.

McCleary, Bryce. Forthcoming. "Queer Folk Linguistics: Language Regard, Identity, and Drag Performers in Oklahoma." In *Linguistics Out of the Closet: The Interdisciplinarity of Gender and Sexuality in Language Science*, edited by Tyler Everette Kibbey. Berlin: Walter de Gruyter.

Miles, Tiya. 2015. *Ties That Bind: The Story of an Afro-Cherokee Family in Slavery and Freedom*. 2nd ed. Oakland, Calif.: University of California Press. https://doi.org/ 10.1525/9780520961029.

Newton, Esther. 1979. *Mother Camp: Female Impersonators in America*. Chicago: University of Chicago Press.

Niedzielski, Nancy A., and Dennis R. Preston. 2003. *Folk Linguistics*. Berlin: Mouton de Gruyter.

Paris Is Burning. 1990. Directed by Jennie Livingston. Miramax Films. 78 min.

Pérez-Milans, Miguel. 2016. "Language and Identity in Linguistic Ethnography." In *The Routledge Handbook of Language and Identity*, edited by Siân Preece, 83–97. London: Routledge.

Pichler, Pia, and Nathanael Williams. 2016. "Hipsters in the Hood: Authenticating Indexicalities in Young Men's Hip-Hop Talk." *Language in Society* 45, no. 4 (Sept.): 557–81. https://doi.org/10.1017/S0047404516000427.

Preston, Dennis R. 1996. "Whaddayaknow? The Modes of Folk Linguistic Awareness." *Language Awareness* 5, no. 1: 40–74. https://doi.org/10.1080/09658416 .1996.9959890.

Preston, Dennis R. 2019. "How to Trick Respondents into Revealing Implicit Attitudes—Talk to Them." In "Implicitness and Experimental Methods in Language Variation Research," edited by Laura Rosseel and Stefan Grondelaers. Special issue, *Linguistics Vanguard* 5, no. s1: art. 20180006. https://doi.org/10.1515/ lingvan-2018-0006.

Rosa, Jonathan, and Nelson Flores. 2017. "Unsettling Race and Language: Toward a Raciolinguistic Perspective." *Language in Society* 46, no. 5: 621–47. https://doi .org/10.1017/S0047404517000562.

Sahlins, Marshall. 2013. *What Kinship Is—And Is Not*. Chicago: University of Chicago Press.

Shetina, Michael. 2018. "Snatching an Archive: Gay Citation, Queer Belonging and the Production of Pleasure in *RuPaul's Drag Race*." *Queer Studies in Media and Pop Culture* 3, no. 2: 143–58. https://doi.org/10.1386/qsmpc.3.2.143_1.

Simmons-Horton, Sherri Y., Tanya N. Rollins, Richard Harris, and Ashley Blackmore. 2022. "Aunties, Uncles, Me Maws, and Play Cousins: Exploring Trends in Formal Kinship Care for Black Families in Texas." *Child Welfare* 100, no. 1: 165–93.

Smitherman, Geneva. 1994. *Black Talk: Words and Phrases from the Hood to the Amen Corner*. Boston: Houghton Mifflin.

Smitherman, Geneva. 2017. "Raciolinguistics, 'Mis-Education,' and Language Arts Teaching in the 21st Century." *Language Arts Journal of Michigan* 32, no. 2 (Spring): 4–12. https://doi.org/10.9707/2168-149X.2164.

Southard, Bruce. 1993. "Elements of Midwestern Speech in Oklahoma." In *"Heartland" English: Variation and Transition in the American Midwest*, edited by Timothy C. Frazer, 229–43. Tuscaloosa: University of Alabama Press.

Stofleth, Daniel, and Valerie Manusov. 2019. "Talking about Mindfulness: An Ethnography of Communication Analysis of Two Speech Communities." *Language and Communication* 67 (July): 45–54. https://doi.org/10.1016/j.langcom.2018.12.003.

Thomas, Erik R. 2001. *An Acoustic Analysis of Vowel Variation in New World English.* Publication of the American Dialect Society 85. Durham, N.C.: Duke University Press. https://read.dukeupress.edu/pads/issue/85/1.

Tillery, Jan, and Guy Bailey. 1998. "*Yall* in Oklahoma." *American Speech* 73, no. 3 (Fall): 257–78. https://doi.org/10.2307/455825.

Walters, Suzanna Danuta. 2012. "The Kids Are All Right but the Lesbians Aren't: Queer Kinship in US Culture." *Sexualities* 15, no. 8 (Dec.): 917–33. https://doi.org/10.1177/1363460712459311.

Weinraub, Clarece D. C. 2015. "Influences of African American English That Contribute to the Exclusion of African American Students from Academic Discourse." Ed.D. diss., University of Southern California.

Weirich, Phillip. 2013. "Watching Hawks and Hocks: A Study of Vowel Mergers in Oklahoma." M.A. thesis, Oklahoma State University.

Zentella, Ana Celia. 2018. "LatinUs and Linguistics: Complaints, Conflicts, and Contradictions—The Anthro-political Linguistics Solution." In *Questioning Theoretical Primitives in Linguistic Inquiry: Papers in Honor of Ricardo Otheguy*, edited by Naomi L. Shin and Daniel Erker, 189–208. Amsterdam: Benjamins.

Zimman, Lal. 2020. "Transgender Language, Transgender Moment: Toward a Trans linguistics." In *The Oxford Handbook of Language and Sexuality*, edited by Kira Hall and Rusty Barrett. Oxford: Oxford University Press. https://doi.org/10.1093/oxfordhb/9780190212926.013.45.

BRYCE McCLEARY is a lecturer in linguistics at Rice University. Their research focuses on language and identity, particularly concerning gender and sexuality. Their research often centers around language regard data to highlight the voices of LGBTQ+ communities, their awareness of language, and the important role language plays in navigating increasingly difficult cultural terrain in the United States. Email: bryce.mccleary@rice.edu.

THE INFLUENCE OF ENGLISH ON NEOLOGISMS FOR NONBINARY GENDER IDENTITIES AND SEXUAL ORIENTATIONS IN QUEBEC FRENCH: BETWEEN VARIATION AND PURISM

MIREILLE ELCHACAR

Université TÉLUQ

ABSTRACT: This article creates a portrait of recent designations of nonbinary gender identities and sexual orientations in Quebec French. It addresses how purism and the condemnation of anglicisms played a part in this vocabulary. The most frequent neologisms in the French press in Quebec are *LBGT** and *queer*. The Office québécois de la langue française (OQLF), Quebec's official language institution, first condemned *queer* because of Quebec's sensitive history with anglicisms and created *allosexuel* and *altersexuel* to replace it. However, these terms were found to be artificial and were not very successful, bringing the OQLF the change its initial normative judgment on *queer*, which is now accepted. More than the negative attitude toward anglicisms in Quebec, what played a major role in the circulation of those neologisms is the need for traditionally dominated groups to gain symbolic power by choosing their own labels, especially those used in a variety of languages worldwide, strengthening the sense of identity and belonging of historically marginalized groups and individuals.

KEYWORDS: anglicisms, queer theory, redenomination, symbolic power

SINCE THE BEGINNING of the twenty-first century, the growing need to take into account the diversity of nonbinary gender identities and sexual orientations has brought its share of neologisms to the French language (Greco 2015; Lorenzi 2017). Some of those neologisms stay mostly inside LGBT*[1] communities or groups (e.g., *pansexuel, bigenre, agenre*), whereas others have been taken up by the general press (e.g., *queer, trans, LGBT* and its different forms) (Laprade 2014; Elchacar and Salita 2018). Some have made their way into professional French dictionaries, including the digital *Le Petit Robert de la langue française* (2023) and *Usito* (Elchacar 2019), seen by some as the "ultimate consecration" (Pruvost and Sablayrolles 2003, 121).

These neologisms were not created in order to name a new reality, but rather by changes in perception, an evolution in cultural mores. From the

American Speech, Vol. 98, No. 1, February 2023 DOI 10.1215/00031283-10579455

Bourdieu (2001) theoretical point of view, these new designations are an attempt to gain symbolic power by the main stakeholders (the dominated) through words, first in their own inner circles and ultimately in mass media. The distinctive terms that existed prior to the year 2000 (*gay, lesbienne, homosexuel*) adhere to a binary view of sexual orientation and gender identity. The neologisms offer nonbinary labels for each paradigm (sexual orientation: *pansexual*; gender identity: *bispirituel, trans*), sometimes for both in a single word (*LGBT*, queer*). These neologisms testify to "the adoption of identity labels by social groups to increase recognition" (Petit 2012, 5; my translation).[2]

This article analyzes gender identity and sexual orientation neologisms that have entered Quebec French and are used in the general press. Two major forces particularly influence the adoption of a neologism by the speech community in Quebec French: diatopic variation in uses and norms, and attitudes toward borrowings, more specifically anglicisms.

The neologisms that emerged in this lexical field are not all the same throughout French-speaking communities. This article analyzes the factors behind the creation of some Quebec French neologisms and the reasons why the speech community did not adopt them. It offers an explanation as to why the most frequent ones in the general press are the same in Quebec and in France, even when they are borrowed from English, which is often a barrier to use in the written press or formal speech in Quebec French. It begins by explaining Quebec's history with anglicisms.

ANGLICISMS IN QUEBEC FRENCH: A HISTORICAL EXPLANATION TO CONTEMPORARY PERCEPTIONS AND BEHAVIORS

The historical context in which French Quebec began borrowing English words helps us understand the reaction Quebecois have toward anglicisms today. Like many languages around the world, French has been borrowing English words mainly since the eighteenth and nineteenth centuries, first from British and then from American English. However, not only are those borrowings not always the same in France and in Quebec,[3] but the judgments cast upon anglicisms are not the same. This brings us back to the speech community as defined by Labov (1989, 2): "The speech community has been defined as an aggregate of speakers who share a set of norms for the interpretation of language, as reflected in their treatment of linguistic variables: patterns of social stratification, style shifting, and subjective evaluations." Members of a speech community share similar judgments on speech practices: what is considered as formal, poor, derogatory, and so on. In general, the Quebec French speech community does not judge anglicisms in a positive way. Anglicisms used in informal speech tend to be replaced in more formal contexts with French equivalents created by the Office Québécois de la langue française (OQLF), Quebec's official linguistic institution, for that purpose. In France, anglicisms are generally neutral and can be used in speech that is more formal (Bouchard 1989; Forlot 2010; Loubier 2011).

This difference is due to the way in which those borrowings historically began, and, according to sociolinguist Chantal Bouchard (1999, 2008), by the social class of those who first did the borrowing. In France, English borrowings began in the eighteenth century; they were made by the upper class who had the financial means to travel to Great Britain. There was a sense of admiration toward advances in the Industrial Revolution and, in the eighteenth-century Enlightenment, toward the political and legal domains. While France was still under Divine Right Monarchy, the British had introduced parliamentary monarchy, with elected members. In the legal field, the English introduced notions such as the *jury*, where one was judged by a body of peers. When the French explained these notions, they did so by borrowing the English words (Steukardt 2006).[4] This admiration eventually escalated to everything British—a phenomenon that has been called Anglomania (Grieder 1985). One extreme illustration is that of faux anglicisms, French words with an English appearance, often with an English suffix, without attestation in English (e.g., *recordman* 'n. record holder', *footing* 'n. light jog'). This practice was mostly active in France during the latter half of the 1800s and the first half of the 1900s, even though some such creation are attested in Quebec French (e.g., *brushing*, a hairdressing term meaning 'n. blow-dry').

Unlike in France, which was never under British rule, English borrowings first entered Quebec French in the context of British control over the colony.[5] Further borrowing resulted from direct contact between Quebec French and English. From the eighteenth century to the first half of the nineteenth century, anglicisms were borrowed by the uneducated French-speaking proletariat who worked in British-owned factories, and later in American-owned ones. Anglicisms take over whole lexical fields where the French terminology is unknown or does not yet exist in Quebec: trade, business, pulp and papers, and later on the automobile industry (Auger 2002; Maurais 2008).[6] Adding to the negative perception toward these borrowings is the fact that they penetrate Quebec French through oral and written speech, whereas they came to be in France mainly through written speech, perceived as more prestigious (Côté and Remysen 2019).

The root of the negative perception of anglicisms in Quebec French is to be found in this particular context of political and economic domination:

This perception is the result of the unequal balance of power between the French and English languages in Quebec (and more broadly in Canada and North America). Associated with political and economic domination, at least until the adoption of French as the sole official language of the province of Quebec in 1977, English was considered an invader, and French had to be preserved from its harmful influence. [Côté and Remysen 2019, ¶5; my translation][7]

This penetration of anglicisms in Quebec French is perceived as one of the reasons for the language's "degradation," as sociolinguist Shana Poplack explains:

[M]ost people, laypeople as well as linguists, ascribe this to one or both of the following reasons: 1) separation from the European metropolis, where the language has supposedly remained in its pristine state, and 2) long-term contact with English, the majority language in most of the country. These are thought to have caused the minority language to lose its distinctive traits, while imposing other, English-origin features that contravene the spirit of the French language. [Poplack 2009, 119]

This combination of factors contributed to linguistic insecurity as defined by Labov (1966): a dichotomy felt by native speakers between their ideal of a standard language and their actual linguistic competence.

The linguistic situation began changing around the Révolution tranquille ('Quiet Revolution')[8] of the 1960s, when the Quebec French population saw the improvement of their socioeconomic status and the increase of their schooling rates. Linguistic laws were passed to protect and promote French at school, in the workplace, and in public display. The government founded a linguistic institution, the Office de la langue française (precursor of the present-day OQLF), with the intention of creating French words to replace English borrowings.

Anglicisms did not altogether disappear from Quebec French, but they are now generally reserved to informal speech, being associated with poor language ability or errors. Oakes and Peled (2018, 120) give an example with the object 'fan': in Quebec French, this object can be named with the anglicism *fan* or with the French word *ventilateur*, but in reality "francophone Quebecers would avoid using the word *fan* in formal contexts as well, because the word belongs to an informal register in Quebec."

Even though the socioeconomic and linguistic situation has changed substantially in Quebec since the 1960s, negative connotations accompany anglicisms to this day. Sociolinguist Olivia Walsh confirms this through a survey on purist attitudes and behaviors in France and Quebec: "The results of the study show that, contrary to expectations, the French respondents display only mild purism and the Québécois respondents are more purist in the face of English borrowings (external purism)" (2014, 423).

The historical context pertaining to the penetration of anglicisms in France and Quebec French explains many differences. First, even though all French-speaking communities borrow English words, they are not always the same.[9] The anglicisms *babysitter, magnet,* and *ferry* are used in France but not in Quebec; conversely, *insécure,*[10] *joke,* and *wiper* are used in Quebec but not in France. Second, the French equivalents suggested by each community to replace anglicisms are not always the same, the main reason for this being that each community has its own official linguistic institution—la Délégation à la langue française et aux langues régionales de France[11] and l'Office Québécois de la langue française. That is why the anglicism *hashtag,* used in both varieties of French, is translated by *mot-clic* in Quebec and *mot-dièse* in France. Third, as mentioned before, the general attitude toward anglicisms is not the same: *babysitter, magnet,* and *ferry* are considered neutral in France, whereas *insécure, joke,* and *wiper* are considered as mistakes in Quebec and replaced by French words in more formal contexts (Walsh 2014; N. Vincent 2015). Thus, the Quebec press has widely adopted *mot-clic,* while the French still use *hashtag* far more frequently than *mot-dièse* (Elchacar 2017). One emblematic example is the word *courriel,* which has replaced the anglicism *email* in the written language and formal speech in Quebec, while *email* is still widespread in France (N. Vincent 2014). Walsh (2014, 441–42) comes to the same conclusion through her survey: "They [Quebecois respondents] were also more likely to choose terminology commission terms, which may suggest that the promotion and implantation of such terms is more widespread in Quebec than in France."

The prescriptive norm regarding anglicisms is particularly strong in Quebec French, which explains some of the neologisms that were proposed by the OQLF to name sexual diversity. However, it is not the only force at work to determine whether people will continue to use an anglicism or turn to the French equivalent suggested by the OQLF. The following analysis shows how identity issues sometimes have the upper hand.

NEOLOGISMS TO NAME SEXUAL ORIENTATIONS AND GENDER IDENTITIES IN QUEBEC FRENCH

The starting point of this analysis are the neologisms designating gender identities and sexual orientations found in three glossaries: (1) the glossary of the Fédérations des enseignantes et enseignants du Québec (Dubuc

2017), published by the teachers' union as an educational tool, (2) the *Wiktionnaire*'s (2011–) "Vocabulaire LGBTIQ en français," a crowdsourced nonprofessional online glossary on the French version of the *Wiktionary*, and (3) the "Glossaire des termes LGBT," published by the Rainbow Project (2012), an educational tool created by the European Union. These glossaries were created because traditional dictionaries' descriptions of gender identity and sexual orientation were seen as falling behind, incomplete, or inadequate (Elchacar 2019). Their nomenclature is more comprehensive than that of general dictionaries, and they cover both Quebec and Europe, which makes them an interesting choice.

The neologisms found in those glossaries were looked up in Eureka (https://eureka.cc), an online database that contains full-text newspaper and magazine articles in French and English from Canada and other countries. Eureka's search engine enables users to search for texts published in a specific language, in a specific category (e.g., publications in French-speaking Canada or Europe), and for a specified time frame. The Eureka search was limited to the written press (print or online), excluding television and radio, social media, studies and reports, and directories and profiles. Words are considered neologisms if they were first found in Eureka after the year 2000, except for *queer*, which is first documented in 1996 (explained later). Table 1 shows the list of neologisms found in Eureka in at least 20 articles. (The words only appear in French, since a translation in English for each word does not always exist.)

The neologisms in the top three positions, *LGBT**, *queer*, and *trans*, are used both in European and Canadian Frenches. The first two, *LGBT** and *queer*, can be linked back to the English language.[12] It is not surprising to find anglicisms in Quebec French, bearing in mind its proximity with the English language, particularly in Montreal (Planchon 2018). What is surprising is that no French equivalent has replaced these anglicisms in frequency in the written press, considering Quebec's difficult relationship to anglicisms in more neutral or formal speech.

The most frequent neologism by far is *LGBT* and its variants. Although the letters first referred to English words (*lesbian, gay, bisexual, transsexual*, or *transgender...*), they were reinvested with the French equivalents: *lesbienne, gay, bisexuel, transsexuel*, or *transgenre*. Second-place *queer* is a regular anglicism that has kept its written form and, in Quebec, retains its English pronunciation with a retroflex [ɹ], absent in French.

The fact that they are influenced by English does not seem to have an impact on the adoption of these neologisms. The initialism *LGBT** is used by many LGBT* defense and support groups in Quebec, whether it appears directly in the group's name (e.g., Conseil Québécois LGBT, which used to

TABLE 1

Frequency and Year of First Appearance of Neologisms Naming Sexual
Orientation and Gender Identity in the French Canadian Press

Year of the First Appearance in Eureka	Neologism[a]	Frequency[b] in French Canadian Press (through Feb. 2, 2022)
2002	LGBT*[c]	27,799
1996	queer	6,123
—[d]	trans	4,642
2002	bispirituel	637
2013	cisgenre[e]	413
2002[f]	pansexuel	229
2002	allosexuel	287
2015	asexuel	229
2003	altersexuel	45
2013	agenre	32

a. We searched for all the forms of a word when it applied (masculine, feminine, singular, plural).
b. Eureka gives the number of documents (articles) in which these words were found—not the number of occurrences of the words, so each word could be used more than once in each document.
c. We launched our search with the form <LGBT*>. In Eureka, an asterisk acts as a wild card, thus finding occurrences of the word *LGBT* as well as its extended variants (*LGBTQ, LGBTQ2, LGBTQ2+*, etc.).
d. *Trans* has many homonym forms and is found in many expressions, such as *gras trans* 'trans fats' or in proper nouns such as *TransCanada* (train), *Trans Mountain* (pipeline), and many others. We searched for collocations of the word *trans* with the meaning relevant to our study: *personne(s) trans, femme(s) trans, homme(s) trans, enfant(s) trans, adolescent(s) trans, parent(s) trans, individu(s) trans, identité(s) trans*. This makes it difficult to find the exact first occurrence in the meaning at study here. However, it is absent from all dictionaries prior to 2000, and many metalinguistic comments accompany it in the press. This is why we classified it as a neologism.
e. The neologism *cisgenre* (*cisgender* in English), though it refers to a person who identifies with the gender assigned at birth, in other words the dominant group, is a way to reassign this group within the same paradigm, using the same morphological pattern. In English, "Cisgender began circulating in online transgender discussion groups in the mid-1990s" (Cava, 2016), and was popularized by Serano (2007). We therefore decided to integrate it in our analysis.
f. *Pansexuel* appears in only one document each in the years 2002, 2005, and 2011; it becomes more frequent in 2012.

be called Conseil Québécois des gais et lesbiennes; Coalition des familles LGBT) or in the description of the group's mission (e.g., GRIS, Jeunesse j'écoute). It is also the appellation used in governmental publications and websites. One reason behind the success of this abbreviation may be that it attempts to encompass all genders and sexual identities: it is an umbrella term, and the plus or asterisk following the initials is an effort to include everyone—even those who do not identify with the letters present in the variant of the abbreviation being used. Official institutions can see this as a means to ensure that everyone feels included.

Despite its success and its all-inclusive potential, *LGBT** is not the only neologism used in French. Similarly to *LGBT**, some neologisms are relatively frequent and used throughout French-speaking communities, such as *queer* and *trans*. Others are limited to the American or the European continent. This raises the issue of geographical variation in the French language.

DIATOPIC VARIATION IN SEXUAL ORIENTATIONS AND GENDER IDENTITIES NEOLOGISMS

Three neologisms in table 1 are particular to Quebec French: *allosexuel, altersexuel,* and *bispirituel.* These words all have a link with the English language: *allosexuel* and *altersexuel,* which we will look at in the next section, are suggestions approved by official linguistic institutions to replace the anglicism *queer. Bispirituel* is a translation of the English word *two-spirit,* which is itself a translation of a concept used by certain First Nations communities to name a nonbinary gender identity.

BISPIRITUEL: A WORD ROOTED IN NORTH AMERICAN INDIGENOUS COMMUNITIES. No professional French dictionary[13] or resource has proposed an etymology for *bispirituel* to our knowledge. The *Wiktionnaire* gives this information in the etymology section: "(1990) Calque from the English two-spirit, from the ojibwé niizh manidoowag expression, meant to replace bardache, considered as an insult" (my translation).[14]

Bardache (and its variant *berdache*) is a derogatory term. *Merriam-Webster .com* dictionary gives the following etymology: "American French, alteration of French *bardache* catamite, from Italian dialect (southern Italy) *bardascio,* from Arabic *bardaj* slave, from Persian *bardag* prisoner, from Middle Persian *vartak*" (s.v. BERDACHE, accessed Oct. 12, 2022; cf. Lo Vecchio 2022). The word is, however, not frequent in contemporary Quebec French. We do not find it in French Canadian dictionaries. It is present in less than 50 documents on Eureka.

First Nations communities replaced *bardache* with *two-spirit.*

This term was chosen to fulfill two functions: first, to replace the highly problematic colonialist term *berdache,* which was previously used throughout anthropology and related fields for Native American third- and fourth-gender roles; and second, to provide a new term that might encompass all of the localized realizations of indigenous gender and sexual variance in North America. [Davis 2014, 65]

This information appears in our corpus, for example, in this article published in the newspaper *Métro*:

> 1. Alors, ils ont créé le terme «two-spirited» (bispirituel) [NDLR: qui est une traduction du terme Anishinaabeg niizh manidoowag, qui fait référence à une personne qui possède à la fois un esprit masculin et féminin] pour connecter leurs cultures autochtone et LGBT ensemble.
> 'They [LGBT Indigenous communities in Manitoba] created the term "two-spirited" (bispirituel) [editor's note: which is a translation of the Anishinaabeg term niizh manidoowag, in reference to a person who possesses both a masculine and a feminine spirit] to connect the Indigenous and LGBT cultures together.'
> [Laurence Houde-Roy, "Qui sont les bispirituels?" *Métro*, Aug. 10, 2016, https://journalmetro.com/actualites/national/1006631/qui-sont-les -bispirituels/; annotation in original]

Its anchoring in the First Nations communities of North America explains why the word is almost absent of the European press and professional French dictionaries, such as *Le petit Robert.* In Quebec, it is attested in the *Grand dictionnaire terminologique* (*GDT*), an online terminology database produced by the OQLF. It is nonetheless not very frequent in mainstream media compared to the neologisms at the top three positions. It often appears with metalinguistic remarks, such as an explanation or definition, as in example 2, or with its English translation, as in example 1:

> 2. Il explique qu'être bispirituel représente une identification spirituelle et, en même temps, une identité sexuelle et de genre, hors des catégories créées par la société prédominante.
> 'He [Blake Desjarlais] explains that being two-spirits represents a spiritual identification as well as a sexual and gender identity, outside the categories created by the dominant society.'
> [Boris Proulx, "Diversité aux Communes," *Le Devoir*, Oct. 9, 2021, B5]

The fact that *bispirituel* is a term brought to Quebec French through the English language is never presented as a prescriptive issue in the corpus. Two possible explanations are that it is linked to the Indigenous peoples of

Canada and that it is not an English word per say, having been borrowed by English from local languages. Other words from North American Indigenous languages made a stop in English before arriving in French, such as *tipi* (*teepee*), *wigwam,* or *mohawk.* Contemporary French Canadian dictionaries do not present these words as criticized anglicisms, and no French equivalent are suggested to replace them.

Not surprisingly, *bispirituel* is almost always found in articles concerning First Nations communities or matters:

> 3. Bispirituel sert à qualifier le lien spirituel qui unit les personnes LGBTQ+ autochtones à leurs familles, communautés et nations.
> 'Two-Spirit is used to describe the spiritual connection that unites Indigenous LGBTQ+ people to their families, communities, and nations.'
> [Patrimoine canadien, Gouvernement du Canada, "La ministre Chagger participe au lancement virtuel d'un projet financé à même le Fonds de développement des capacités communautaires LGBTQ2 au Manitoba," *Canada NewsWire,* May 6, 2021; http://www.newswire.ca/fr/releases/archive/May2021/06/c5931.html]
> 4. Le terme «bispirituel» est utilisé par certaines personnes autochtones pour décrire leur identité sexuelle, spirituelle et de genre.
> 'The term *Two-Spirit* is used by some Indigenous people to describe their sexual, spiritual and gender identity'
> [Kijâtai-Alexandra Veillette-Cheezo, "La signification de la baleine bleue sur mon tambour," ICI Radio-Canada, Espaces autochtones, Jan. 18 2021, https://ici.radio-canada.ca/espaces-autochtones/1855251/signification-baleine-bleue-tambour-bien-etre-bi-spiritualite]

This is a case of a doubly dominated group: LGBT* groups are dominated by binary gender identity and traditional sexual orientations; two-spirit people are also dominated as First Nations groups in a White-dominant culture: "As individuals marginalized in multiple ways, Two-Spirits must differentiate themselves not only from heteronormative and gender-normative Natives, but also from nonindigenous GLBTIQ people with whom they may also at some level identify" (Davis 2014, 62–63).

Bispirituel is sometimes incorporated to the *LGBT* initialism, *LGBT2S,* where the "2S" stands for 'two-spirit'. In its "Lexicon of Terminology," the National Inquiry into Missing and Murdered Indigenous Women and Girls puts forward the "preferred term" 2SLGTBQQIA, with the following explanation:

> 5. By putting "2S" at the front, we are remembering that Two-Spirit people have existed in many Indigenous Nations and communities long before other understandings of gender and orientation came to us through colonization.

This also puts Two-Spirit people right at the front of our conversations, rather than at the end.[15] [Nov. 1, 2018, https://www.mmiwg-ffada.ca/wp-content/uploads/2018/02/NIMMIWG_Lexicon_ENFR-1.pdf]

The scope of *Two-Spirit* is explained as being as wide as *queer*, the two being umbrella words.

Bispirituel is the only word specific to Quebec French that is still being used in the general press.

TRANSPÉDÉGOUINE: A WORD ROOTED IN THE EUROPEAN CONTINENT. Research in other francophone communities mention neologisms that are not used in Quebec, such as *transpédégouine*, a portmanteau of *trans*, *pédé*, and *gouine*, created by LGBT groups in France (Lorenzi 2017; Welzer-Lang 2018). As it is the case for *queer*, *transpédégouine* is an attempt to empower LGBT groups and individuals by reclaiming words that were first intended as insults and incorporating them in a denomination: *gouine*, a derogatory term for *lesbian*, and *pédé*, a derogatory term used in France for *gay*. We found *transpédégouine* in only two articles published in the French Canadian sources on Eureka, each in reference to France:

6. En France, on peut lire parfois le néologisme « *transpédégouine* », qui reproduit cette même réappropriation de l'insulte.
   'In France, we sometimes read the neologism "transpédégouine," which demonstrates the same reappropriation of the insult.'
   [Sophie Chartier, "*Queer*, un flou clair pour les minorités sexuelles," *Le Devoir*, July 20, 2017, A5]

One possible reason why *transpedegouine* is not used in Quebec is the incorporation of the insult *pédé*, a francism not used in Quebec—it is not in the *Usito*, the contemporary general dictionary of North American French. The offensive word *gouine*, however, is also in use in Quebec, but it has not been reclaimed in contexts of empowerment.[16]

But the fact is that Quebec no longer looks to France to legitimize its use of the French language. While the Quebec French linguistic norm historically tried to align itself with Parisian French (Lockerbie 2003; Cajolet-Laganière 2021), an emancipation movement started in the 1960s with the Révolution tranquille (Mercier, Remysen, and Cajolet-Laganière 2017). In 1985, the Office de la langue française published its *Énoncé d'une politique linguistique relative aux québécismes*, clearly putting forward an endogenous norm for Quebec French that has been called Français québécois standard ('Quebec standard French'): "This standard, which is part of the language planning process of Quebec, must take into account the sociocultural and sociolinguistic contexts of Quebec, its geographic location and its belonging to the Francophonie" (§2.1; my translation).[17]

Today, this autonomy from the French norm manifests itself in many ways. As we saw previously, French communities each have their own official institutions that make recommendations, which results in differences in the specialized terms each region uses. (A chiropractor is called *chiropraticien* in Quebec and *chiropracteur* in France; in Quebec, a *radiologiste* is a doctor, whereas a *radiologiste* in France can be either a doctor or a technician, and the word *radiologue* is also used in France, but not in Quebec.) This linguistic emancipation also manifests itself through lexicography (Mercier 2008), Quebec being the first French-speaking community outside France to write a general dictionary based on its own uses and norms (*Usito*).[18] Another example is feminization: Quebec French has been using feminine forms for titles and professions for decades, whereas France still mainly uses the masculine (Vachon-L'Heureux 2004; Arbour and Nayves 2014). This explains why Anne Hidalgo is *maire* of Paris and Valérie Plante is *mairesse* of Montréal (in 2022).

Quebec French also follows its own standard and normative decisions regarding anglicisms. The other neologisms under study that are used only in Quebec, *allosexuel* and *altersexuel,* are French equivalents approved by the OQLF to replace the anglicism *queer.*

THE ANGLICISM *QUEER*: AT THE CROSSROAD BETWEEN IDENTITY AND NORMATIVE ISSUES

The fact that *queer* is a straightforward anglicism that keeps its English appearance and pronunciation in French may explain why the OQLF proposed French equivalents, *altersexuel* and *allosexuel,* to replace it while not suggesting any for *LGBT*.* Because the fates of these French equivalents are linked to *queer,* we searched for their frequency over time in Eureka to verify whether the French equivalents had any effect on the vitality of *queer.* We also added *LGBT** to this diachronic analysis, as it is the most frequent neologism. We started our search in 1996, the year *queer,* the oldest neologism in the French Canadian sources on Eureka, first appeared. The results, displayed in figure 1, clearly show that the French equivalents are very rare, not imposing themselves over time, whereas the frequency of *queer* and *LGBT** has risen steadily.

It is only with its meaning linked to the LGBT* movement that the anglicism *queer* was adopted in French. Its presence in French is relatively recent, and its use in the general press remained low until 2012 (Laprade 2014).

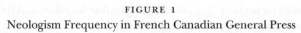

FIGURE 1
Neologism Frequency in French Canadian General Press

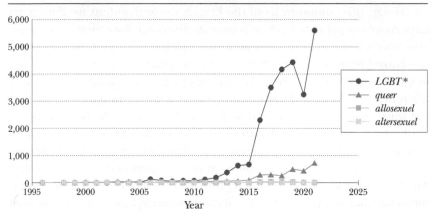

The word began circulating in the media during 1990s; it was then used in proper nouns of groups or events (*Queer Notion, Queer Comics, le Festival Queer City, Queer as Folk*). The first occurrence of *queer* as a common noun is in 1996:

> 7. Face au mouvement d'émancipation de la culture *queer* des dernières années, cette production paraît s'inscrire en faux.
> 'This exhibition [*Poisons/Phobia*, by artist Phillipe Raphanel] seems contrary to the liberation of queer culture in recent years.'
> [Bernard Lamarche, "Les fondements de la différence," *Le Devoir*, Oct. 12, 1996, D8]

Use of *queer* becomes more widespread in 2016, when popular singer Coeur de pirate came out as queer on social media following the Orlando nightclub shooting. The word, then, was seemingly unknown by ordinary speakers:

> 8. C'est fou comme les choses ont changé! Dix-neuf ans plus tard, Coeur de pirate fait son coming out dans une longue lettre ouverte et utilise le terme «queer» qui laisse bien du monde perplexe, y compris Jasmin Roy![19]
> 'It's crazy how things have changed! Nineteen years later, Coeur de pirate comes out in a long letter and uses the word *queer*, puzzling quite a few people, including Jasmin Roy!'
> [Sophie Durocher, "Le placard de Coeur de pirate," *Le Journal de Montréal*, June 20, 2016, https://www.journaldemontreal.com/2016/06/20/le-placard-de -cur-de-pirate]

In French, sensitivity to the word *queer* does not arise from its initial pejorative usage—which may well be unknown to most French speakers—

but rather from the fact that it is an English word. Inevitably, the arrival of a new anglicism brought up the usual normative questions: Is it acceptable to use this borrowing? Could we not find a French word to use instead? In an interview, a member of a LGBT* defense group explains:

> 9. Parce qu'il signifie tout ce qui n'est pas hétérosexuel, le terme anglais *queer* plaisait beaucoup aux dirigeants, mais devait être francisé.
> 'Because it means everything that is not heterosexual, the directors [of Regroupement d'entraide pour la jeunesse allosexuelle du Québec] liked the English word *queer* very much, but it had to be Frenchified.'
> [Presse Canadienne, "Fini les gais, les lesbiennes, les bisexuels, vive les allosexuels," *Le Devoir*, June 14 2002, A10]

The OQLF proposed two French equivalents to replace *queer* in 2015 through its *Grand dictionnaire terminologique* (*GDT*): *allosexuel* and *altersexuel*. The *GDT* presents lexicographical information for each term on a separate page, including judgments on the acceptability of any associated anglicisms and their official French equivalents. Prior to 2019, *queer* did not have its own entry in the *GDT*. When someone looked for the word *queer* in the *GDT*, they would be taken automatically to the entry for *allosexuel*: the definition and note for *allosexuel* were marked with a green checkpoint to indicate they are prescriptively correct to use: they were presented as "termes privilégiés" ('preferred terms') to replace the anglicism *queer*. *Queer* was mentioned at the bottom of the page and classified as an error.[20]

The sheet for *allosexuel* presented a short definition ("is said of that which concerns sexual orientations other than heterosexual"), followed by this explanation: "The term *allosexuel* is formed with the prefix *allo-* which means 'of a different nature'. It was invented to translate the English word *queer*."

It is the Regroupement d'entraide à la jeunesse allosexuelle du Quebec (REJAQ), which was active from 2002 to 2008, that first suggested the neologism *allosexuel* (Laprade 2014), going so far as to include the word in its name.

> 10. C'est d'ailleurs en collaboration avec les autres membres du regroupement qu'Hugo Valiquette a créé le mot «allosexuel», afin d'unifier les différentes orientations et identités sexuelles sous un même terme rassembleur.
> 'In collaboration with other members of the group [REJAC], Hugo Valiquette created the word *allosexuel* in order to unify different sexual identities and orientations under a single unifying term.'
> [Geneviève Quessy, "Hugo Valiquette reçoit le Prix Honoris," *L'Action week-end* (Joliette), Nov. 3, 2013, 32]

The choice of the prefix *allo-* was seen as fit to name all that did not fall into binary gender identity and sexual orientation:

> 11. «Le préfixe allo- devenait donc intéressant pour désigner tout ce qui s'écarte de la majorité hétérosexuelle», poursuit-il.
> '"The prefix *allo-* seemed like a good way to designate all that differs from the heterosexual majority," he [REJAC teasurer Jean-Pierre Lord] added.'
> [Presse Canadienne, "Fini les gais, les lesbiennes, les bisexuels, vive les allosexuels," *Le Devoir,* June 14 2002, A10]

The appearance of *allosexuel* in the corpus is linked to its creation by REJAC. Only 287 documents with the word come up through a search in all French Canadian sources, including 30 documents where *allosexuel* is mentioned in the name of a group.[21] *Allosexuel* often appears between quotation marks or followed by a definition, both indications that the word is new or might be unknown or unclear to the reader. The few other occurrences found in the press are mostly metalinguistic. Either journalists present the new word (as in 12) or they openly admit that they looked it up to avoid using the anglicism *queer* (as in 13):

> 12. Adieu les gais! Fini les lesbiennes! Plus jamais de bisexuels! Tous sont mainte-nant allosexuels. Le Regroupement d'entraide pour la jeunesse allosexuelle du Quebec (REJAQ) désire faire adopter ce néologisme plus inclusif pour faire tomber toutes les étiquettes collées aux minorités sexuelles.
> 'Farewell gays! No more lesbians! No more bisexuals! All are now queer. The REJAQ wishes to have this more inclusive neologism adopted to break down all the labels attached to sexual minorities.'
> [Presse Canadienne, "Le REJAQ désire faire tomber les étiquettes collées aux minorités sexuelles," *Cyberpresse,* June 13, 2002]
> 13. J'ai commencé par me tourner vers l'Office de la langue française, qui affirme que «queer» peut se traduire par «allosexuel».
> 'I first looked to the OQLF, which states that *queer* can be translated as *allosexuel*.'
> [Sophie Durocher, "Coeur de queer," *Le Journal de Montréal,* June 17, 2016, 46]

Allosexuel is sometimes followed by *queer,* a sign the author did not think the word would be transparent for the reader and that *queer* would:

> 14. La communauté allosexuelle (queer) autochtone a fait cela avec la bispiritualité.
> 'The allosexuelle community did this with two-spirits.'
> [Laurence Niosi, "Bispiritualité : se réapproprier son identité de genre," *ICI Radio-Canada,* Nov. 11 2017, https://ici.radio-canada.ca/nouvelle/1066392/bispirituel-autochtone-gai-two-spirit-sommet]

According to Laprade (2014, 4), who did a semiotic study on the word *queer* but who also worked in an LGBT* defense group, this French equivalent was mostly used by academics and institutions looking for a French word to use in official documents, questionnaires, and so forth. He also admits in an interview to the press that it was not taken up by LGBT* groups or by the general population:

> 15. Chez nous, le mot «allosexuel» est accepté par l'Office de la langue française en guise de traduction pour queer. Mais cette traduction n'a pas la même force de frappe, note Bruno Laprade [...]. «*Le mot n'a pas remporté de véritable succès dans la population.* [...]»
>
>   'Here, the word *allosexuel* is accepted by the OQLF as a translation for *queer*. But this translation does not have the same impact, notes Bruna Laprade [...]. "The word has not been a success among the population. [...]"'
>
>   [Sophie Chartier, "*Queer*, un flou clair pour les minorités sexuelles," *Le Devoir*, July 20, 2017, A5]

The other French equivalent proposed by the OQLF is *altersexuel*, which had its own entry in the *GDT* in 2015 that was shortly thereafter (2017) combined with the *allosexuel* entry, though *altersexuel* did not appear in the headword for the entry.

Altersexuel uses the same radical *sexuel* but this time with the fractomorpheme *alter-*. The notion of fractomorpheme was first introduced by Tournier: "A fractomorpheme is a part of a lexeme which represents this lexeme in a complex word" (Tournier 1985, 86; my translation).[22] Fractomorphemes differ from prefixes in that they represent the meaning of a whole word in a fragment of it used to form a new word. One common example is *e-* when it conveys the whole meaning of 'electronic', such as in *email* or *ecommerce*. Though fractomorphemes are more productive in English, they do exist in French (see Fradin 2000; Humbley 2012; Elchacar 2016).

Altersexuel is used even less often than *allosexuel*: only 45 documents use the word in all of French Canadian documents found on Eureka to this day. It is not used in the name of a group, which seems to have helped *allosexuel* circulate. Quotation marks accompany the word in four documents, and a definition follows it in 10. The prescriptive pressure toward repression of anglicisms is perceptible: we find occurrences of *altersexuel* in parentheses following *queer* as clarification, even though *queer* is the more frequent and understood term:

> 16. On y aborde même le mouvement queer (altersexuel)!
>
>   'Even the queer movement is discussed!'
>
>   [Marie-Pier Frappier, "Télévision à la une—Un homme sur deux est une femme," *Le Devoir*, Mar. 3, 2012, 3]

There are signs that journalists try to integrate the French equivalents to *queer* yet know that the words are not understood by the public:

17. Jeune diplômé du Conservatoire d'art dramatique de Montréal, Charles Voyer ne voit pas le genre d'un personnage comme une barrière. [...] «[...] Mon approche est davantage performative, altersexuelle [*queer*], donc voulant échapper à la catégorisation genrée. [...]»
    'A young graduate of the Montreal Conservatory of Dramatic Arts, Charles Voyer does not see a character's gender as a barrier. "My approach is more performative, queer, therefore wanting to escape gender categorization."'
    [Marie Labrecque, "Changer de sexe sur scène," *Le Devoir*, Feb. 1, 2020, D5; bracketed *queer* in original]
18. À la fois galerie d'art et studio, Penrose Studio propose une approche collective, marginale (underground) et altersexuelle (queer).
    'Both an art gallery and a studio, Penrose Studio offers a collective approach, unconventional and queer.'
    [Céleste Godin, "Tout simplement différent," *Acadie Nouvelle*, Apr. 25, 2017, 6]
19. Dans sa lettre, elle se présente comme «queer», un terme parfois traduit par «allosexuelle» ou «altersexuelle» et qui inclut les «personnes dont l'orientation sexuelle est autre qu'hétérosexuelle», selon l'Office québécois de la langue française.
    'In her letter, she introduces herself as "queer", a term sometimes translated as *allosexual* or *altersexual* and which includes "people whose sexual orientation is other than heterosexual", according to the Office québécois de la langue française.'
    [Presse Canadienne, "Coeur de pirate «sort du placard»," *Le Droit*, June 17, 2016, 26]

LGBT* defense groups have not adopted these French equivalents—except for the *Regroupement d'entraide à la jeunesse allosexuelle du Quebec*, which no longer exists. Figure 1 above shows that despite its English origins, *queer* is still used in the general press, while use of its French equivalents *altersexuel* and *allosexuel* has lessened. Conversely, *LGBT*, queer,* and *trans* are less and less accompanied by metalinguistic marks, remarks, or definitions. In a glossary of LGBT* terms presented in the newspaper *La Presse+* in 2016, under the word *queer*, the journalist paraphrases Marie-Pier Boisvert, who was at the time the director of the Quebec LGBT Council; Boisvert claims that *queer* does not have any convincing French equivalents and that *allosexuel* and *altersexuel* remain rare.

20. Sans équivalent convaincant en français—allosexuel ou altersexuel demeurent peu utilisés—, *queer* n'est pas un synonyme de bisexuel.
    '*Queer*, which lacks a convincing French equivalent—*allosexuel* and *altersexuel* are not much used—is not synonym for *bisexual*.'
    [Alexandre Vigneault, "Lexique LGBTQ," *La Presse+*, Aug. 9, 2016, 4]

In the following extract, Laprade explains that *allosexuel* does not have the same impact as *queer* and questions the French language's inclusive potential:

21. «[...] *L'adoption du mot* queer *parle beaucoup de notre américanisation et des limites du français à rendre compte de ses fondements sexistes. Les langues fonctionnent par incorporation. Il n'y a pas de raison pour laquelle le français ne pourrait pas inclure le mot* queer *dans son vocabulaire sans avoir à le traduire*», répond le jeune chercheur.
'"The adoption of the word *queer* speaks of our Americanization and of the French language's sexist foundations. Languages work by incorporation. There is no reason why French should not include *queer* in its vocabulary without having to translate it," responds the young researcher.'
[Sophie Chartier, "*Queer*, un flou clair pour les minorités sexuelles," *Le Devoir*, July 20, 2017, A5]

So why not simply use the abbreviation *LGBT**, which works both in French and in English? Because *queer* confers a different meaning: "'queer' does not name some natural kind or refer to some determinate object; it acquires its meaning from its oppositional relation to the norm" (Halperin 1995, 62). This is also the idea expressed here by Boisvert:

22. S'afficher comme *queer*, c'est à la fois s'opposer à la «conformité hétéro-sexuelle» et «aux lettres LGBT». Le terme *queer*, mal compris même au sein de certaines communautés LGBT, selon Marie-Pier Boisvert, porte en lui-même le désir de transgresser les limites imposées par le genre.
'Claiming one is queer is a way of opposing oneself to heterosexual conformity and to the letters LGBT. The term *queer*, sometimes misunderstood even in certain LGBT communities, carries the desire to transgress gender-imposed limits, according to Marie-Pier Boisvert.'
[Alexandre Vigneault, "Lexique LGBTQ," *La Presse+*, Aug. 9, 2016, 4]

We therefore find ourselves at the intersection between two forces at work, both trying to influence a speech community's use of words: identity on one side, particularly identity of marginalized groups, and language prescriptivism on the other. It appears that in this case, the will for a group to choose its own designation is stronger than the will to conform to a certain standard of French where anglicisms are (mostly) frowned upon. In this particular case, the proposition of the OQLF was not adopted by the general population nor by LGBT* groups. One possible explanation is that *queer* fills a gap in the French lexicon: no other word is as inclusive as well as deliberately vague (Elchacar and Salita 2018). Another reason is that many other speech communities, not only English-speaking ones, use *queer*:

23. Pour Silver Catalano, le terme, bien précis, a tellement été adopté qu'il peut être compris partout dans le monde.
'For [singer song-writer] Silver Catalano, the term [*queer*] has been adopted so widely that it is understood around the world.'
[*Le Devoir*, 17 juillet 2017]

As a result, the OQLF changed its judgment toward *queer* and admitted that the two French equivalents proposed, *allosexuel* and *altersexuel*, did not meet the expected success. Now when one searches for the word *queer* in the *GDT*, revised in 2019, they are taken to the entry for *personne queer* 'queer person'.[23] This time the "termes privilégiés" are *personne queer* and *queer*, with the green checkmark informing the user that this is the preferred term from the OQLF's prescriptive point of view, and the two French "equivalents" *allosexuel* and *altersexuel* are placed in another section at the bottom of the sheet called "termes utilisés dans certains contextes" ('terms to be used in certain contexts'). What is particularly interesting in this entry are the comments for *queer* and for *allosexuel* and *altersexuel*. First, about *queer*, the *GDT* says, "The term *queer* is acceptable because it is legitimized in Quebec French and other French communities. Moreover, it is used in other languages."[24] The *GDT* mentions the international scope of the word. The note referring to the French equivalents mentions: "The terms *allosexuel* and *altersexuel*, which the OQLF had proposed, did not implement themselves in the French language. Furthermore, according to some experts, the terms *allosexuel* and *altersexuel* only partially designate *queer* because the element *-sexuel* generally expresses the idea of a sexual orientation whereas *queer* can also refer to gender identity."[25]

This outcome is an illustration that usage by the speech community is the "ultimate arbiter of borrowing behavior," as Poplack (2018, 214) puts it: "Community norms are the primary determinant of propensity to borrow altogether, and they also dictate the preference for nonce borrowing over lexical retrieval of established loanwords." Official institutions can only make suggestions to replace an anglicism with a French equivalent. Even if most French equivalents are undertaken by the speakers and replace anglicisms, at least in formal speech, some simply are not. The reason may be that the anglicism was introduced a long time ago and is well implanted (e.g., *leader*), because it does not come across as an "error" or as less formal by the prescriptive norm (e.g., *muffin*, *camping*) or because the French equivalent does not seem well formed in French (e.g., the spelling *coquetel* instead of *cocktail*). In the case of *queer*, the main reasons for accepting it is that LGBT* groups themselves have asserted its importance, given that no other word conveys exactly the same meaning and that it is used in many languages and LGBT* communities around the world (Prearo 2015).

CONCLUSION: A CHANGE OF PARADIGM?

If prescriptive pressure and sensitivity toward anglicisms are very strong in Quebec, they are not the only forces at work to determine if a neologism will make its way in general discourse. Even if Quebec tends to follow its own linguistic standard, particularly regarding anglicisms, and generally adopts the French equivalents approved by the OQLF, it was not the case this time. The opinions of LGBT* groups toward the neologisms seem to have played an important role in their circulation, more so than the negative attitude toward anglicisms in Quebec French.

The need for Quebec's LGBT* groups to connect with other LGBT* groups around the world, which have also adopted the neologisms *queer* and *LGBT**, also plays a part in the terms' distribution. The choice of moniker becomes a means for marginalized groups to join a wider, international movement. As Divita and Curtis (2019, 6) point out in their study of the anglicism *coming out* as used in the French magazine *Têtu*: "a loanword may spread and change over time, gaining potency in its symbolic function as a marker of belonging to the sociocultural realm that its use and meaning conjure." For LGBT* communities, which are not part of the dominant group, the use of the same words worldwide allows them to join forces with other LGBT* communities around the world, be they English-speaking or communities that have also incorporated these anglicisms in their language. *LGBT**, *queer*, and *trans* make it possible to transcend languages and cultures in order to strengthen the sense of identity and belonging of historically marginalized groups and individuals.

The only neologism specific to Quebec French that continues being used is *bispirituel*. In this case, the Quebec French specificity is accepted not because of prescriptive preoccupations but because of the need to take into account the reality of First Nations communities.

NOTES

Ada Luna Salita helped gather and analyse the press corpus. Svetlana Komarova helped gather the dictionary corpus. I wish to thank them for their assistance.

1. In this article, the form *LGBT** is used so as not to exclude shorter forms. The asterisk is a reminder that the abbreviation can be expanded with letters, numbers, and symbols (e.g., *LGBTQ2+*).
2. "[…] l'appropriation identitaire de dénominations par des groupes sociaux, à desfins de reconnaissance" (Petit 2012, 5).

3. For the purpose of this article, we will concentrate on French as spoken in France (more specifically Paris) and Quebec, though many more geographical varieties of French exist.

4. Another example is sports vocabulary, where English gave many loanwords to French (Rosoff 1981).

5. Borrowing from English into Quebec French continued under the Anglophone government once Canada shifted from monarchy to Commonwealth rule.

6. The automobile industry in France does not have anglicisms because it developed independently, with its own French terms.

7. "Cette perception est le résultat du rapport de force inégalitaire des langues française et anglaise au Québec (et plus largement au Canada et en Amérique du Nord) : associée à la domination politique et économique, à tout le moins jusqu'à l'adoption du français comme seule langue officielle du Québec dans les années 1970, l'anglais est considéré comme l'envahisseur et il faut préserver le français de ses influences néfastes" (Côté and Remysen 2019, ¶5).

8. The Quiet Revolution is a time of rapid social and economic change in the province, which also influenced the French language and its representations (Lockerbie 2003).

9. This is especially the case for more recent borrowings. Anglicisms borrowed in the nineteenth century, at a time when Quebec still looked to France to legitimize its usage, are present in both French-speaking communities (e.g., *leader*, *building*, *cocktail*) and considered neutral.

10. Some anglicisms adopt French morphological aspects, such as an accent, as it is the case with *insécure*. Anglicisms in Quebec can also be morphologically derived, creating a new word from an anglicism. For example, the anglicism *cancel* is conjugated as a French word, with French morphemes: *canceler*, *cancelé*, and so on.

11. Contrary to a received idea, the Académie française does not hold any power over the French language other than historical and symbolic.

12. We can suppose that this may also be the case with *trans*, which comes in third place in table 1, although I am not able to completely verify this hypothesis. The only professional dictionary which has an entry for *trans* is *Le Petit Robert*; the etymology is vague (20th century, abbreviation). However, the etymology section in the *Wiktionnaire* gives this information: "Apocope de *transsexuel* ou *transgenre*" (accessed Oct. 12, 2022); that is, the word is an apocope of the English words—the words in French are *transsexuel* and *transgenre*. This can easily be translated in French, meaning *trans* can be the apocope of both the English and the French words. The English word *trans* may well have had an influence on the French word *trans*.

13. I make a distinction between professional dictionaries, written by professional lexicographers, and nonprofessional dictionaries, be they crowdsourced, collaborative, or written by nonlexicographers (see Sajous, Josselin-Leray, and Hathout 2018).

14. "*(1990)* Calque de l'anglais *two-spirit*, de l'expression ojibwé *niizh manidoowag* pour remplacer *bardache*, considéré insultant" (*Wiktionnaire*, s.v. BISPIRITUEL, last updated Sept. 20, 2022).

15. There is, however, a lexical field typical to Quebec French in which words are stripped of their initial meaning in an attempt to regain power: the sacres, which are curse words appropriated from the vocabulary associated with the Catholic church and the celebration of mass (e.g., *tabernacle, ostie* 'host', *calice* 'chalice'), at a time when the Church was omnipresent in Quebec. For a linguistic study of this question, see D. Vincent 1982; Dostie 2015.

16. "Cette norme, qui s'insère dans le processus d'aménagement linguistique du Québec, doit tenir compte du contexte socioculturel et sociolinguistique du Québec, de sa situation géographique et de son appartenance à la francophonie" (Office de la langue française 1985, §2.1).

17. Although French in Quebec and Canada has a rich lexicographical history, with dictionaries of a differential approach or adaptations of dictionaries published in France to North American or Quebec French (*Dictionnaire du français Plus* 1988; *Dictionnaire québécois d'aujourd'hui* 1992). Many initiatives of a normative approach have also been published, the most popular being the *Multidictionnaire* (Villers 1988). However, *Usito*, first published in 2013, is the first general dictionary of French as spoken in Quebec with an entirely original description.

18. The emphasis on two-spirit people is not maintained in the National Inquiry into Missing and Murdered Indigenous Women and Girls chosen French term, *LGBTAB* ("personne lesbienne, gaie, bisexuelle, transgenre, allosexuelle et bispirituelle") (https://www.mmiwg-ffada.ca/wp-content/uploads/2018/02/NIMMIWG_Lexicon_ENFR-1.pdf).

19. Jasmin Roy is an actor and host in Quebec where he is also known for his work against bullying in schools, including that directed toward LGBT* youth.

20. The Office québécois de la langue française did not grant permission to duplicate the entry for *allosexuel* in this article.

21. The most frequent group being the REJAQ, but Projet alliance allosexuelle-hétérosexuelle is also in the corpus.

22. "Un fracto-morphème est donc un fragment de lexie qui la représente dans un mot construit" (Tournier 1985, 86).

23. It is worth noting that the expression *personne queer* is not very frequent, appearing in only 143 documents in all Eureka sources.

24. "Le terme *queer* est acceptable parce qu'il est légitimé en français au Québec et ailleurs en francophonie. De plus, il est employé dans plusieurs langues" (*GDT*, s.v. PERSONNE QUEER).

25. "Les termes *allosexuel* et *altersexuel*, que l'Office québécois de la langue française avait proposés, ne se sont pas implantés. Par ailleurs, pour certains spécialistes, les termes *allosexuel* et *altersexuel* ne désignent que partiellement le présent concept, puisque l'élément *-sexuel* exprime généralement l'idée d'une orientation sexuelle, alors qu'il est aussi question ici d'identité de genre" (*GDT*, s.v. PERSONNE QUEER).

REFERENCES

Arbour, Marie-Ève, and Hélène de Nayves. 2014. "Féminisation linguistique: Étude comparative de l'implantation de variantes féminines marquées au Canada et en Europe." *Langage et société*, no. 148, 31–51. https://doi.org/10.3917/ls.148.0031.

Auger, Pierre. 2002. "Le phénomène de l'anglicisation de la langue forestière au Québec: Essai de socioterminologie diachronique." In *Mélanges offerts à Jean-Louis Fossat* (Cahiers d'études romanes, nouvelle série, 11/12), edited by Lídia Rabassa, 39–56. Toulouse, France: Centre de linguistique et de dialectologie, Université de Toulouse-Le Mirail.

Bouchard, Chantal. 1989 "Une obsession nationale: L'anglicisme." *Recherche sociographiques* 30, no. 1: 67–90. https://doi.org/10.7202/056408ar.

Bouchard, Chantal. 1999. *On n'emprunte qu'aux riches: La valeur sociolinguistique et symbolique des emprunts.* Montreal: Fidès.

Bouchard, Chantal. 2008. *Obsessed with Language: A Sociolinguistic History of Quebec.* Toronto: Guernica.

Bourdieu, Pierre. 2001. *Langage et pouvoir symbolique.* Paris: Éditions Fayard.

Cajolet-Laganière, Hélène. 2021. "L'essor d'une norme endogène au Québec: L'exemple du dictionnaire Usito." *Gragoatá* 26, no. 54: 105–38. https://doi.org/10.22409/gragoata.v26i54.46376.

Cava, Peter. 2016. "Cisgender and Cissexual." In *The Wiley Blackwell Encyclopedia of Gender and Sexuality Studies*, edited by Nancy A. Naples. Malden, Mass.: Wiley-Blackwell. https://doi.org/10.1002/9781118663219.wbegss131.

Côté, Marie-Hélène, and Wim Remysen. 2019. "L'adaptation phonologique des emprunts à l'anglais dans les dictionnaires québécois." In *Les discours de référence sur la langue française*, edited by Anne Dister and Sophie Piron, 173–95. Brussels: Presses de l'Université Saint-Louis.

Davis, Jenny L. 2014. "'More Than Just "Gay Indians"': Intersecting Articulations of Two-Spirit Gender, Sexuality, and Indigenousness." In *Queer Excursions: Retheorizing Binaries in Language, Gender, and Sexuality*, edited by Lal Zimman, Jenny L. Davis, and Joshua Raclaw, 62–80. Oxford: Oxford University Press.

Dictionnaire du français Plus: À l'usage des francophones d'Amérique. 1988. Edited by Claude Poirier. Montreal: Centre éducatif et culturel.

Dictionnaire québécois d'aujourd'hui: Langue française, histoire, géographie, culture générale. 1992. Edited by Jean-Claude Boulanger, Jean-Yves Dugas, and Bruno de Bessé. Saint-Laurent, Que.: Dicorobert.

Divita, David, and William Curtis. 2019. "The Life of a Loanword: A Case Study of *le coming out* in the French Magazine *Têtu* (1995–2015)." *Ampersand* 6: art. 100053. https://doi.org/10.1016/j.amper.2019.100053.

Dostie, Gaétane. 2015. "Les dérivés verbaux de sacres en français québécois: Sens, positionnement dans le diasystème et synonymes proches." *Cahiers de lexicologie*, no. 107, 185–202.

Dubuc, Dominique. 2017. "LGBTQI2SNBA+ Les mots de la diversité liée au sexe, au genre et à l'orientation sexuelle." Fédération des enseignantes et des enseignants du Québec (FNNEQ-CSN). https://fneeq.qc.ca/wp-content/uploads/Glossaire .pdf.

Elchacar, Mireille. 2016. "Étude diachronique de néologismes du vocabulaire socio-politique: La vitalité de *antimondialisation, altermondialiste* et du fractomorphème *alter-* dix ans après leur apparition dans la presse générale." *Neologica*, no. 10, 75–100. https://doi.org/10.15122/isbn.978-2-406-06279-0.p.0075.

Elchacar, Mireille. 2017. "Le traitement lexicographique des anglicismes au vu de la variation géographique: L'exemple de deux outils en ligne." In "Dictionnaires, culture numérique et décentralisation de la norme dans l'espace francophone," edited by Chiara Molinari and Nadine Vincent. *Repères DoRiF*, no. 14.

Elchacar, Mireille. 2019 "Comparaison du traitement lexicographique des appellations des identités de genre non traditionnelles dans les dictionnaires profession-nels et profanes." *ÉLA: Études de linguistique appliquée*, no, 194, 177–91. https:// doi.org/10.3917/ela.194.0177.

Elchacar, Mireille, and Ada Luna Salita. 2018. "Les appellations des identités de genre non traditionnelles: Une approche lexicologique." *Langage et société*, no. 165, 139–65. https://doi.org/10.3917/ls.165.0139.

Forlot, Gilles. 2010. "'Oh là là, ça c'est vraiment de l'anglais!': Discours métalinguis-tiques évaluatifs et processus identitaires en contexte migratoire." *Langage et société*, no. 134, 79–100. https://doi.org/10.3917/ls.134.0079.

Fradin, Bernard. 2000. "Combining Forms, Blends and Related Phenomena." In *Extragrammatical and Marginal Morphology*, edited by Ursula Doleschal and Anna M. Thornton, 11–59. Munich: Lincom Europa.

GDT. Grand dictionnaire terminologique. 2012–. Office québécois de la langue française. https://vitrinelinguistique.oqlf.gouv.qc.ca/. Based on *Banque de terminologie du Québec* (1974); incrementally revised.

Greco, Luca. 2015. "Présentation: La fabrique des genres et ses sexualités." *Langage et société*, no. 152, 7–16. https://doi.org/10.3917/ls.152.0007.

Grieder, Josephine. 1985. *Anglomania in France 1740–1789: Fact, Fiction, and Political Discourse*. Geneva: Librairie Droz.

Halperin, David M. 1995. *Saint Foucault: Towards a Gay Hagiography*. New York: Oxford University Press.

Humbley, John. 2012. "Retour aux origines de la terminologie: L'acte de dénomi-nation." *Langue française*, no. 174 (Aug.): 111–25. https://www.revues.armand -colin.com/lettres-langues/langue-francaise/langue-francaise-ndeg-174-22012/ retour-aux-origines-terminologie-lacte-denomination.

Labov, William. 1966. *The Social Stratification of English in New York City*. Washington, D.C.: Center for Applied Linguistics.

Labov, William. 1989. "Exact Description of the Speech Community: Short *a* in Philadelphia." In *Language Change and Variation*, edited by Ralph W. Fasold and Deborah Schiffrin, 1–58. Amsterdam: Benjamins.

Laprade, Bruno, 2014. "Queer in Québec: Étude de la réception du mouvement queer dans les journaux québécois." *Cygne noir*, no. 2, 93–111. https://doi.org/10.7202/1090759ar.

Le Petit Robert de la langue française. 2023. Version numérique. Paris: Dictionnaires Le Robert.

Lockerbie, Ian. 2003. "Le débat sur l'aménagement du français au Québec." *Globe* 6, no. 1: 125–49. https://doi.org/10.7202/1000696ar.

Lorenzi, Marie-Émilie. 2017. "'Queer,' 'transpédégouine,' 'torduEs,' entre adaptation et réappropriation, les dynamiques de traduction au cœur des créations langagières de l'activisme féministe *queer*." *GLAD!*, no. 2. http://journals.open edition.org/glad/462.

Loubier, Christiane. 2011. *De l'usage de l'emprunt linguistique*. Montreal: Office québécois de la langue française. http://collections.banq.qc.ca/ark:/52327/bs2036402.

Lo Vecchio, Nicholas. 2022. "Revisiting *berdache*: Notes on a Translinguistic Lexical Creation." *American Speech* 97, no. 3 (Aug.): 345–73. https://doi.org/10.1215/00031283-9616142.

Maurais, Jacques. 2008. *Le vocabulaire français au travail: Le cas de la terminologie de l'automobile*. Suivi de la situation linguistique, étude 12. Montreal: Office québécois de la langue française. http://collections.banq.qc.ca/ark:/52327/bs48921.

Mercier, Louis. 2008. "Travailler depuis le Québec à l'émancipation de la lexicographie du français." In *Le français des dictionnaires: L'autre versant de la lexicographie française*, edited by Claudine Bavoux, 289–306. Brussels: De Boeck, Duculot.

Mercier, Louis, Wim Remysen, and Hélène Cajolet-Laganière. 2017. "Québec." In *Manuel des francophonies*, edited by Ursula Reutner, 277–310. Berlin: De Gruyter.

Merriam-Webster.com. 1996–. Springfield, Mass.: Merriam-Webster. https://merriam-webster.com. Originally based on *Merriam-Webster's Collegiate Dictionary*, 10th ed. (1993); incrementally revised.

Oakes, Leigh, and Yael Peled. 2018. *Normative Language Policy: Ethics, Politics, Principles*. Cambridge: Cambridge University Press.

Office de la langue française. 1985. *Énoncé d'une politique linguistique relative aux québécismes*. Montreal: Gouvernement du Québec.

Petit, Gérard. 2012. "Présentation: La dénomination." *Langue française*, no. 174 (June), 3–9. https://www.revues.armand-colin.com/lettres-langue/langue-francaise/langue-francaise-ndeg-174-22012/presentation-denomination.

Planchon, Cécile. 2018. "Anglicismes dans la presse écrite: Le bilinguisme de milieu peut-il expliquer l'anglicisation?" *Journal of French Language Studies* 28, no. 1 (Mar.): 43–66. https://doi.org/10.1017/S0959269517000047.

Poplack, Shana. 2009. "What Language Do We Speak?" *The Trudeau Foundation Papers* 1: 117–39. http://www.sociolinguistics.uottawa.ca/shanapoplack/pubs/articles/Poplack2009TrudeauENG.pdf.

Poplack, Shana. 2018. *Borrowing: Loanwords in the Speech Community and in the Grammar*. New York: Oxford University Press.

Prearo, Massimo. 2015. "La naissance de la formule 'LGBT' en France et en Italie: Une analyse comparative des discours de mobilisation." *Cultures et conflits*, no. 97, 77–95. https://doi.org/10.4000/conflits.18956.

Pruvost, Jean, and Jean-François Sablayrolles. 2003. *Les néologismes*. Paris: Presses universitaires de France.

Rainbow Project. 2012. "Glossaire des termes LGBT." Centro d'Iniziativa Gay Milano. http://www.rainbowproject.eu/material/fr/glossary.htm.

Rosoff, Gary H. 1981. "Anglo-Americanisms in the French Sporting Vocabulary." *Foreign Language Annals* 14 no. 5 (Dec.): 403–6. https://doi.org/10.1111/j .1944-9720.1981.tb01659.x.

Sajous, Franck, Amélie Josselin-Leray, and Nabil Hathout. 2018. "The Complementarity of Crowdsourced Dictionaries and Professional Dictionaries Viewed through the Filter of Neology." *Lexis: Journal of English Lexicology*, no. 12. https://doi.org/ 10.4000/lexis.2322.

Serano, Julia. 2007. *Whipping Girl: A Transsexual Woman on Sexism and the Scapegoating of Femininity*. Berkeley, Calif.: Seal Press.

Steukardt, Agnès. 2006. "L'anglicisme politique dans la seconde moitié du 18e siècle: De la glose d'accueil à l'occultation." *Mots: Les langages du politique*, no. 82, 9–22. https://doi.org/10.4000/mots.746.

Tournier, Jean. 1985. *Introduction descriptive à la lexicogénétique de l'anglais contemporain*. Paris: Champion.

Usito. 2013–. Edited by Hélène Cajolet-Laganière, Pierre Martel, and Chantal-Édith Masson. University of Sherbrooke. https://usito.usherbrooke.ca/. French-language dictionary based on Quebec lingusitic corpora; incrementally revised.

Vachon-L'Heureux, Pierrette. 2004. "Féminisation des titres et des textes." *Correspondances* 10, no. 2 (Nov.). https://correspo.ccdmd.qc.ca/document/reformes-et -continuites/feminisation-des-titres-et-des-textes/.

Villers, Marie-Éva de. 1988. *Multidictionnaire des difficultés de la langue française*. Montreal: Éditions Québec/Amérique.

Vincent, Diane. 1982. *Pressions et impressions sur les sacres au Québec*. Montreal: Office de la langue française, Gouvernement du Québec.

Vincent, Nadine. 2014. "Organismes d'officialisation, dictionnaires et médias: Le triangle des Bermudes de la francisation." In "4e Congrès mondial de linguistique française, Berlin, Allemagne, 19–23 Juillet 2014," edited by Franck Neveu, Peter Blumenthal, Linda Hriba, Annette Gerstenberg, Judith Meinschaefer, and Sophie Prévost. *SHS Web of Conferences* 8: 1731–40. https://doi.org/10.1051/ shsconf/20140801315.

Vincent, Nadine. 2015. "Comment réagit l'usage face à une norme imposée? Évaluation de la réception des recommandations officielles françaises et québécoises dans un corpus journalistique belge et suisse." In "Bulletin VALS-ASLA: Normes langagières en contexte," edited by Johanna Miecznikowski, Matteo Casoni, Sabine Christopher, Alain Kamber, Elena Maria Pandolfi, and Andrea Rocci. *Bulletin suisse de linguistique appliquée* 2015, special issue 1: 149–61. https://doc .rero.ch/record/256995/.

Walsh, Olivia. 2014. "'*Les anglicismes polluent la langue française*': Purist Attitudes in France and Quebec." *Journal of French Language Studies* 24, no. 3 (Nov.): 423–49. https://doi.org/10.1017/S0959269513000227.

Welzer-Lang, Daniel. 2018. *Les nouvelles hétérosexualités.* Toulouse, France: Éditions Érès.

Wiktionnaire. 2011–. "Vocabulaire LGBTIQ en français." Wikimedia Foundation. https://fr.wiktionary.org/wiki/Cat%C3%A9gorie:Vocabulaire_LGBTIQ_en _fran%C3%A7ais. Crowdsourced glossary; incrementally revised.

MIREILLE ELCHACAR is a linguistics professor at Université TÉLUQ and a lecturer at the University of Sherbrooke in Quebec, Canada. Her courses and research focus on lexicology, lexicography, and variation of the French language and address sensitive issues in Quebec French, such as anglicisms, orthography, or new identity labels created by sociopolitical groups. Email: mireille.elchacar@teluq.ca.

YALLAH Y'ALL: THE DEVELOPMENT AND ACCEPTANCE OF QUEER JEWISH LANGUAGE IN SEATTLE

ELLEN PERLEBERG
GRACE ELIZABETH C. DY
LINDSAY HIPPE
University of Washington

ABSTRACT: This study investigates how queer Jewish language develops among LGBTQ Jewish people themselves and the processes by which it is learned and adopted by cis-heterosexual people in shared Jewish spaces, focusing on the influence and perceptions of Seattle as a liberal and queer-accepting city. The authors analyze virtual ethnographic interviews with queer and cis-heterosexual individuals involved in Seattle Jewish life, which discuss participants' experiences and observations surrounding queer Jewish language, emphasizing experiences in learning and adopting queer linguistic features and attitudes toward the acceptance of queer Jewish language in Seattle. It finds that communal awareness and acceptance of queer language in Jewish spaces is largely driven by the presence of queer individuals, particularly in leadership roles.

KEYWORDS: religiolinguistics, Seattle Jewish English, queer religiosity, left coast

THIS STUDY INVESTIGATES the processes by which queer language emerges and is adopted in Seattle Jewish communities, focusing on the compounding marginalization of queerness and Jewishness as it intersects with the perception of Seattle as a "gay city." Intersectionality is a framework which posits that individuals' identities are not discrete but rather mutually constructed and influential (Crenshaw 1987; Levon 2015). Thus, this study approaches queer Jewish identity not as queerness that happens to be Jewish or as Jewishness that happens to be queer, but as a reciprocally informed identity. Moreover, it seeks to investigate how queer Jewish identity is further shaped by the Seattleite identity.

At least 10.7% of Seattle residents identify as LGBT (Balk 2020), and the city has a reputation as queer-friendly and progressive on LGBTQ issues, a phenomenon sometimes identified with the "left coast" (Gregory 2015). Popularly queer, "left coast" cities are frequently cited, accurately or in folk memory, as origins of queer linguistic and semiotic innovations (Smorag 2008). Loughlin (2021) identified a correlation between proximity to queer

American Speech, Vol. 98, No. 1, February 2023   DOI 10.1215/00031283-10579468

culture (e.g., participation in Pride events) and frequent use of singular *they* pronouns for both queer and cis-heterosexual participants; this study predicts that a similar correlation may be evident in speakers' perceptions of their queer language use on a broader sociocultural level as well.

Barringer (2020) identifies that LGB individuals viewed Judaism and non-Evangelical Protestantism as significantly more "friendly/neutral" toward the LGBT+ community, relative to Mormonism, Islam, Catholicism, and evangelical Protestant churches. American Jews tend to be strongly queer-affirming, particularly within the Reform, Reconstructionist, and Conservative movements, and within secular cultural Judaism (Pew Research Center 2013). According to the Pew Research Center (2021), 9% of American Jews identify as lesbian, gay, or bisexual, including 25% of Jews under age 30. The survey did not ask if participants were trans or intersex, so the overall proportion of Jews who are LGBTQ+ is likely higher. Seattle Jews identify primarily as secular or Reform, with smaller Conservative, Orthodox, and Reconstructionist communities, and there is a 40-year history of queer Jewish activism and community-formation in Seattle, visible in events such as annual Pride Shabbat services and "Gay Gezunt!" (a pun on the Yiddish saying *zei gezunt* 'be healthy') held during the Seattle Jewish Film Festival (Boxer et al. 2014). Brennan-Ing et al. (2013) have documented the benefits that LGBT individuals derive from their religious communities, including spiritual and emotional support and opportunities for socialization.

Seattle English is a subdialect of Pacific Northwest English, defined as the primary English dialect of the states of Washington, Idaho, and Oregon. Research on Washington State dialects has emphasized the role of the state's demographic trends and colonization and immigration histories, including the influence of Salishan and other indigenous languages as well as Scandinavian and Asian American Englishes (Wassink 2015). Seattle Jewish language may be described as a variety of Benor's (2009) concept of Jewish English, distinguished from surrounding Englishes by adstrata of Hebrew and diasporic Jewish languages such as Yiddish and Ladino. Notably, Seattle has a large Sephardic Jewish community and "is one of the few cities left in the world with [a] sizeable population of Ladino [Judeo-Spanish] speakers" (FitzMorris 2014, 13).

Queer Jewish language is defined broadly as any language used in Jewish spaces or by Jews through which users produce queer identities or culture (Bucholz and Hall 2005). In Perleberg and Dy (2022), we discuss lexical innovations in contemporary Seattle Queer Jewish English, which incorporated Jewish heritage languages, wordplay, and historical Jewish gender identities (see Kukla 2006) as well as various approaches to navigating the binary gender structure of Hebrew (and Hebrew loanwords). For example, *yallah y'all*, cited by a queer Jewish student in Seattle at a group greeting, combines *yallah* (يلا), an Arabic loanword in Israeli Hebrew (יאללה) meaning 'let's go', with the emergent queer/feminist West Coast English substitution of *y'all* for the (perceived-)gendered *you guys* (Battistella, Denham, and Lobeck 2020).

The present article approaches queer language, and proficiency in it, through analysis of group language practices, such as asking or providing pronouns and their consistent correct use and the adoption of gender-inclusive language in liturgy and other formalized texts. Due to the institutional-level analysis of this article, our definition of queer Jewish language is extended to include language used by cis-heterosexual people to index LGBTQ inclusion. As Hebrew and languages of the Jewish diaspora continue to be used as liturgical and heritage languages, queer Jewish language engages with heteronormativity and the binary gender systems of Hebrew and other Jewish languages as well as English. Queer Jewish groups, such as the Non-binary Hebrew Project (Gross and Rivlin 2021), have developed neologisms and neoforms to accommodate gender-neutral and genderqueer linguistic needs. As the role of Hebrew and other Jewish languages varies throughout Jewish religious and cultural life, this study interprets queer Jewish language as a translingual spectrum representing the full linguistic repertoire of its speakers.

Queer approaches to regional sociolinguistics and other place-based analyses benefit from consideration of social networks (Milroy 1987). Agents with strong ties to the social network can effect language change through cultural power; however, individuals with weaker ties, often through movement or social marginalization, may introduce language change through greater interaction with outside groups. Queer Jewish networks also intersect with "Jewish geography," a custom among many Jews to point out potential mutual acquaintances when meeting. While a well-known cultural phenomenon among Jews (especially Ashkenazi Jews), it is not well represented in linguistic or ethnographic research (Maxwell 2019). Jewish geography represents a cultural test of Milgram's (1967) "small-world experiment" and foments group identification through social networking.

Participation, or lack thereof, in localized queer community networks and activities is a significant factor in queer people's senses of belonging and subsequent adoption of community language (Smorag 2008). Moreover, Loughlin (2021) demonstrates that proximity to queer people (such as through having LGBTQ+ family members or friends or through participation in events such as Pride parades) has a positive effect on cis-heterosexuals' acceptance of singular *they* pronouns, suggesting that strong queer community networks also support queer literacy and allyship among cis-heterosexuals.

METHODOLOGY

Interested individuals were asked to complete a screening form about their involvement in Jewish and LGBT+ life in Seattle. We selected 34 interview participants that reflected a diversity of backgrounds and experiences, including the three researchers who incorporated autoethnographic data into their responses. Interviews were conducted and recorded on Zoom. Interview questions were designed to elicit in-depth self-identification of participants' gender identities and sexual orientations, linguistic backgrounds, and involvement in Jewish life, including participants' negotiation of identity and identity language across social contexts. Interview questions are published in Dy and Perleberg (2022) and are available online as supplemental material to the present article (https://doi.org/10.1215/00031283-10579468). Participants who completed the interview were given a gift card for their time. Interviews were transcribed, and coding schemes were created a posteriori.

Of the 34 participants, 18 identified as LGBTQ+ and 16 did not. Following emergent best practices for linguistic research with LGBTQ+ people, we opted not to quantify participants' descriptions of their genders or orientations in order to avoid conflating the nuances of this self-description, for instance, by replicating fixed gender categories through a male/female/nonbinary "trinary" (Conrod 2020). Participants' pronouns, requested in the preliminary screening survey, were quantified, and while this article does discuss some trends correlating with participants' pronouns, it is important to state that pronouns are not equivalent to gender (e.g., not all people who use *she/her* pronouns identify as women). Eighteen participants used *she/her* pronouns, seven used *he/him*, four used *she/they* or *they/she*, one used *he/they*, and four used *they/them*. No participants used English neopronouns.

The participants hold a variety of roles in the Seattle Jewish community, including rabbis, lay leaders, educators, students, and lay members across a range of religious movements, such as Reconstructionist, Reform, Conservative, Orthodox, and Secular. These participants have been previously or are currently involved with over 16 synagogues, 12 schools and student organizations, and 30 Jewish community organizations in the greater Seattle area. Seven participants were current or former rabbis, two of whom identify as LGBTQ+, and 10 additional participants were currently primarily employed by one or more Jewish organizations (including academic departments in public institutions). Thirty-three participants were native speakers of American English, 14 of whom were native speakers of Pacific Northwest English. One was a native speaker of Israeli Hebrew, and one was a childhood multilingual in English/Israeli Hebrew.

RESULTS AND DISCUSSION

PERCEPTIONS OF SEATTLE AS A QUEER-INCLUSIVE CITY. When asked to evaluate how accepted queer language and culture is in Seattle, cis-heterosexual participants viewed the city as more LGBTQ-friendly than their queer counterparts. A queer lay leader remarked how "Seattle in some ways is actually a little bit behind compared to the New York and San Francisco [Jewish] communities that I'm part of," whereas a cishet educator described Seattle as "ahead of the curve" and received feedback from colleagues across the nation how "Seattle's really out ahead of things, we're not thinking about that here in Florida or Georgia. […] I feel actually pretty good about where Seattle is and that we are overall a very accepting and an open community." Another cis-heterosexual participant recalled how

We have an all-gender bathroom in the synagogue, right, and I said to [my rabbi], "You know, only in Seattle does it just happen." There was no board vote; there was no contentious argument; there was no letter writing; there's nothing, and it just struck me as so wonderful because there are communities that really kind of fall apart over stuff like this, and she's like, "Well, that's not what's important. What's important, you know, SOCIAL JUSTICE is important, the OTHER things are important. It's a toilet, you pee there like why would we fight over that?"

Participants varied in their interpretation of the extent of "the Seattle area." One participant remarked how "in many ways, the city of Seattle, like many cities, once you get outside the city, you're in Alabama." Another participant extended Seattleite progressive values to a broader area of Washington, saying

[If] I'm making a national comparison, I would say that Seattle seems to be like a place that is safe to use, you know, genderqueer language or any kind of language that expresses someone's authentic self, and it doesn't feel like that's a problem or like it's an issue. My child has come out to so many people, like on the street, just like "I'm nonbinary," you know, just like even out in Sequim[1] or like other places out on the [Olympic] Peninsula where you don't– it's not Seattle, and like nobody really bats an eyelash.

Moreover, a queer participant describes how:

Seattle is a nice little bubble in a way. It's a city that has a lot of progressive values, and it really strives to meet those values, so I do feel as though I see a lot of queer language and queer vocabulary and queer culture in Seattle that is perfectly acceptable and accepted and part of the fabric of Seattle. I lived in Capitol Hill when I first lived in Seattle so that could have a bit of a lens for me that I've just always seen Seattle as a queer-accepting and even a queer space itself.

Capitol Hill is a Seattle neighborhood with a large LGBT+ population and has housed several of Seattle's LGBT+ organizations since the 1960s (McKenna and Aguirre 2016). While recognizing the existence and boundaries of queer spaces in Seattle, another cishet participant notes how there are Seattle "neighborhoods that are known for being accepting, but I also have a friend who is a man who was attacked recently on Capitol Hill which was– would be one of the neighborhoods that maybe he would feel safest in, and he was attacked and called by various slurs, and so I know that that exists as well." In June 2015, Seattle's mayor described how sites of homophobic and transphobic assults, along with those of heavy traffic, were later used to determine the location of the 11 rainbow crosswalks that were added to the city (Raghavendran 2015). Echoing the findings of Wolowic et al. (2017), the presence of physical markers utilizing the pride rainbow can serve as a positive indicator about a community but does not necessarily guarantee supportive and inclusive people and practices.

Parallel usage of physical markers as indicators of liberal sociopolitical views is reflected in one cishet participant who noted that "as soon as you leave Seattle, half the time you start seeing trucks and gun racks. It just is completely different." In addition to referencing the physical borders of Seattle, the presence and political symbolism of physical markers such as "trucks and gun racks" was seen as standing in opposition to queer inclusive beliefs and practices. Similarly, some speakers used derogatory stereotypes of Southeastern U.S. states to position themselves and Seattleite identity in contrast to an imagined South, as seen in "once you get outside the city, you're in Alabama" and "I found that's easier for people who don't quite know LGBTQ+ things to understand, especially in Texas." However, external geographic comparisons were not limited to the South, as in, "Plus, it's Seattle. I'm sure if you ask someone like in Phoenix you'd have different answers."

The most positive attitudes toward Seattle among queer participants were held by individuals who had moved to Seattle from areas outside the West Coast:

For someone who's from Seattle, they might kind of feel bad in some ways about Seattle, but for me, in terms of like queer identity specifically, it was definitely the most accepting place I've ever been, and so for me it just seemed so great and open. You know, my partner felt the same way, just because we're both two good old Southern boys, but it was a different experience that we really liked. I mean just seeing churches with pride flags on them? Like that was something that we actually had like culture shock for a minute, because we were not used to things like that, and like we went to Capitol Hill, and you know how they have like the rainbow sidewalks? We were very confused, like we thought it was for a party or a festival that was happening, and we didn't know that's just how it was.

Within the Seattle Jewish community, one cishet rabbi noted how when writing "to the committee in Jerusalem on standards, they always say 'only in Seattle do we get these questions,' because she's had so many questions that most communities are not as halakhicly [*adv.* 'regarding Jewish law'] serious with a wide range of people who belong."[2] A cishet lay staff member noted how:

Most of the gay membership in Seattle that are actually actively gay and actively Jewish come to [our synagogue], so we've had even prior to the Conservative movement allowing for it, there've been gay marriages there because we didn't care, so we've had the gay marriages, we have trans people in our congregation, we have a specifically gender nongender bathroom in case people feel uncomfortable, and we had [a] trans THEM working in our early childhood center.

A rabbi similarly noted how the phenomenon of individual synagogues and people in Seattle making queer-inclusive decisions ahead of movement-wide changes, such as how

The [Reform Rabbis'] manual like didn't have language for same-sex wedding officiation and things like that, and so if I look at my manual, I have chicken scratch of going through and changing all of the Hebrew gendered pronouns and suffixes and all of that. Now the new handbook has all sorts of different options for language, so I think I'm existing at a time where that shift is happening, and I want to say that manual was published in 2014? Maybe '15.

The perception of Seattle as "more progressive" on LGBTQ+ issues may be because Washington State legalized same-sex marriage in 2012, three years before its national legalization through the Supreme Court case *Obergefell v. Hodges*. Similarly, the movement-wide decision to include queer language may follow a long national conversation in America about LGBTQ+ inclusion and marriage, such as the end of California's 2008 Proposition 8 to ban same-sex marriage, "Don't Ask, Don't Tell," the Defense of Marriage Act, and the Supreme Court cases *United States v. Windsor* (2013) and *Obergefell v. Hodges* (2015).

PERCEPTIONS OF QUEER INCLUSION IN SEATTLE JEWISH LIFE AND LANGUAGE. As a religious heritage language, Hebrew is used by many Jews in prayers and religious services, emphasizing the need for gender-neutral and queer-inclusive language in liturgy. Twenty-seven participants perceived the grammatical gender binary of Hebrew as more difficult to make queer-inclusive than English, often citing the use of English singular *they* pronouns and other less gendered options such as *folks* instead of *ladies and gentlemen*. One queer participant describes how:

When the language that surrounds the religious [or] spiritual aspect of your community is inherently gendered, it's really hard to get away from that. In my understanding of, say, some Christian organizations where they don't use Latin or they don't use Hebrew and it's all English, it's much easier to use more sensitive or specific queer language, which is not possible if you're saying *baruch atah Adona* [ברוך אתה אלוהינו] like it's no matter what, 'Blessed are you, God' is male male male.

Participants reported fluidity of participation and engagement across Reform, Conservative, Reconstructionist, Independent, and secular Jewish organizations, with the notable exception of Orthodox life. One participant self-identified as "probably the most connected with Jewish organizations of anyone in Seattle, the only thing is I don't have any contact with Orthodox organizations." One nonbinary participant recalls how "when I'm in an Orthodox space, I present as a cisgender man because that's what safest. There's no room for queerness or gender identity or anything like that in more Orthodox or Conservative spaces… Orthodoxy is really built around gender and tradition, so in places like that I really let my queer identity fall to the back and become quote unquote fully Jewish." Two cis-heterosexual Orthodox participants recalled how conversations about LGBTQ+ topics are understood as "private choices that people make" rather than communal issues, as "people [are] not ready to deal with it in the [Orthodox] synagogue context." For these individuals, examples of queer-inclusive language in Jewish spaces were found only in public educational settings and in multimovement community organizations. The notable exception to this general lack of engagement across Seattle Orthodox and Reform/Conservative communities were queer Sephardic Jews, who were interested in connecting to their heritage through attending a Sephardic synagogue but were uncomfortable with the presence of the mechitza, partitions separating men's and women's spaces, in these Orthodox communities (Perleberg and Dy 2022).

SIGNALING QUEER-AFFIRMATION IN JEWISH SPACES. Self-selection into affirming/queer spaces was a common theme among queer participants, occuring both interpersonally and institutionally. One queer participant said, "When I got to college and started meeting about a million queer people, and all my high school friends started BECOMING all these queer people, then ((laughs)) yeah that's how it works," while another described their process of self-selection as "if [a local queer rabbi]'s giving a drashah ['sermon'], I know [they're] not going to be like 'homosexuality, you're gonna burn in hell,' or whatever, right? ((laughs)) Like there's that degree of safety in that."

One cishet rabbi described trying to "find ways to continuously say out loud that we are LGBTQ+ friendly and inclusive," such as through the placement of pride stickers on their doors. While these indicators may be useful, no participants cited this as an indicator of queer safety and inclusion in a Jewish space. One queer lay leader critiqued that these physical visuals are not enough and proposes cultural and behavioral shifts.

> I would like to see a greater commitment to explicit creating of safe spaces through queer language from the organizations themselves. Not just on the website, I don't want it to just be like a little side thing or just like it's good to have a [pride] flag; it's good to have some kind of indication on your homepage of the website first of all that like says this is a safe place for people with all kind of gender... Make all the rabbis put their pronouns on their [email signatures], let all the people who cisgendered people who are in positions of power in the Jewish community just say what pronouns they are because it really makes a difference to create spaces like that and... That's like a free freaking easy, two-second thing that everyone could do like that just doesn't take anything away from anyone and can create a lot of safety.

Open opportunities to share one's pronouns, such as through introductions, email signatures, and Zoom display names, were widely cited as indicators of queer inclusion within an organization, particularly during COVID-19 (Dy and Perleberg 2021). Standardization of this practice has been met with some resistance, such as one queer participant recalls in response to a request to "get pronouns on name tags please. We're queer; this is really important to us. A lot of people were like okay YOU can put pronouns on YOUR name tag which... wasn't fostering inclusivity."

As predicted, attitudes toward the relationship between Jewish movements and queer language proficiency mirrored those toward other communities seen as progressive, such as the city of Seattle. One participant addressed this challenge, noting, "I know that Reform doesn't necessarily always mean inclusive and vice versa?" One of the most frequently cited factors in being queer-affirming was the presence of openly queer clergy and staff. The role of religious movement is particularly important here, as the Reform movement's Central Conference of American Rabbis allowed full inclusion of queer rabbis and lay members in 1990 and the Conservative movement's Committee on Jewish Law and Standards allowed for the ordination of queer clergy in 2006 (Human Rights Campaign 2015). Many participants noted the connection between the relatively recent development of the ordination of queer individuals in the past 15–30 years as being influenced by the perception and role of women and femininity in Judaism. In addition to the theological implications of gendering God beyond utilizing *He/Him* pronouns, both clergy and lay members noted how the ordination of women paved the way for movement-wide conversations about gender and sexuality. One queer lay leader recalls how:

The Reform movement was pretty progressive with like LGBTQ awareness and language. I think that a lot of it had to do with, not the language of gender in the sense of expansive awareness of gender as a spectrum, but including the fact that there are women who are leading prayers, and it doesn't want to have just be so patriarchal all the time. It wasn't even nonbinary at all; it was just like not trying to be male-dominated or patriarchal. Since then, there's been so many shifts in the community as far as how we refer to God and how we can change our prayer language so it's not so narrow and how we use Hebrew, which is a very binary gendered language, to be more inclusive and more universal for all people.

In addition to queer clergy, the presence of queer lay members also contributed to the sense of safety and comfort in Jewish spaces. One participant recalls feeling more "fully comfortable existing as a trans person there [which] was helped also by older trans people or older LGBT people who existed at [my synagogue]." This pattern is also observed by cis-heterosexuals. When trying to find a synagogue to attend, one queer participant recalls "playing Jewish geography with [a cishet colleague] like 'Oh, my friend who's a lesbian goes here' and so self-selecting into safe spaces with other queer people."

QUEER JEWISH LANGUAGE TRANSMISSION. This networking and identification of queer leaders in the Jewish community may be seen as an extension of "playing Jewish geography." One participant described Seattle as a "small town"; thus, there are "a lot of people who are four- or five-, six-generation [Seattlites that are] really connected, and a lot of them are related to each other, so Jewish geography is pretty interesting, particularly in the Seattle area." While none of the questions asked participants to specifically name any individuals in the Seattle Jewish community, we observed patterns in who was being cited in the creation and adoption of queer Jewish language (Milroy 1987).

As demonstrated in figure 1, eight participants specifically named two queer clergy members as both teachers of queer Jewish language and indications of queer-inclusion in the Seattle Jewish community. Additionally, four queer lay members, all of whom identify as genderqueer and two of whom are educators, were cited by eight participants regarding their perceived inclusion, known challenges, and as sources of knowledge.

Five cis-heterosexual members of the Jewish community—two rabbis, two language instructors, and one organization leader—were named as gatekeepers of queer language practices (Shoemaker and Vos 2009). While these individuals' impacts were described as largely positive, as sources of knowledge and for their ability to affect institutional change, three queer participants noted how one individual's lack of knowledge around LGBTQ+ hindered their inclusion in that particular space.

FIGURE 1

Dissemination of Queer Jewish Language and Best Language Practices

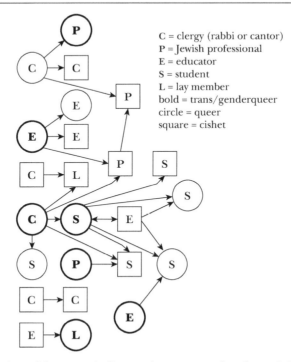

C = clergy (rabbi or cantor)
P = Jewish professional
E = educator
S = student
L = lay member
bold = trans/genderqueer
circle = queer
square = cishet

NOTE: The direction of the arrow indicates who was named as the recipient of the knowledge (i.e., the knowledge was named as originating from those on the left side and is transmitted rightward)

Proximity to queerness was also a significant motivator to learn Queer Jewish language. Changing societal visibility and acceptance of "out" queer individuals made resources to facilitate this learning more available, which also increased learner motivation. Unlike other cultural vocabularies and sociolinguistic cues learned from an early age at home, parents were not frequently cited as the earliest source of learning about queer issues. Rather, as queer identity and expression develops into one's adolescence and adulthood, often nonbiological communities of practice become foundational sources of knowledge (Milton 2020). Twelve queer participants cited themselves as initiators of queer-inclusive change and education, having previously done extensive self-reflection and education. A positive correlation was found between the extent of outness, especially among genderqueer individuals, and communal recognition of their knowledge around queer issues. The known impact and importance of being out is detailed by one queer rabbi, who describes how when they are in spaces "with students and with individuals who are young adults and [while] I present queerly anyhow, I do intentionally go into those spaces using *they/them* pronouns along with *she/her* but [do so] for the sake of visibility, for the sake of letting them know they're not alone [and] to greater emphasize the diversity in faith communities." The impact of out lay members, while different than clergy, was also named, as when one queer participant recalled how "people are starting to [be] like, oh, here she comes again," referencing her role initiating conversations about LGBTQ+ issues such as pronoun inclusion during introductions.

QUEER JEWISH LANGUAGE LEARNING CONTEXTS. In addition to noting who is transmitting queer Jewish language, it is similarly important to note the contexts and roles in which such interactions take place. While most knowledge originates from members with significant visibility, such as clergy and educators, many of whom cited self-reflection and their professional work as their primary sources of learning, the interconnectedness of various settings and learning contexts reflected in Jewish geography challenges traditional learning hierarchies. For example, while the genderqueer student at the center of figure 1 notes learning from a queer clergy member in a religious context, this knowledge, including vocabulary, grammatical innovations, and textual knowledge, was then brought into a secular language classroom, wherein the student was cited by both the instructor and peers.

As reflected in table 1, 82% of participants learned queer language in educational settings, through both formal content in the curriculum (e.g., in middle school health classes and college gender and sexuality courses) and informal conversations with queer educators and peers surrounding identity. Schools were often the first site of exposure to queer vocabulary, although in alignment with Bronfenbrenner's (1995) notion of PROXIMAL PROCESSES, this education continues throughout one's life, in greater depth and in additional contexts, such as in the workplace and in religious life (Renkert 2005). Unlike synagogues and youth groups that are affiliated with a particular movement, educational settings, such as university classes and student organizations, were the greatest point of social interaction across religious movements. Educators in particular recalled learning new vocabulary from their students as well as observed cultural shifts such as in acceptance of trans students and adoption of their pronouns by their peers. One participant redefined the scope to community engagement more broadly, describing how:

People who are [...] actively involved in fields of work in which it is specifically you trying to help the public, like [the] education sector or working for the government, oftentimes have more opportunity to learn how to be welcoming of queer people

TABLE 1

Sources of Queer (Jewish) Language Learning

Learning Context	Frequency	Example Quotations
Education Settings[a]	82% (n = 28)	When I was in high school, I was the founding president of my school's Gay Straight Alliance, so a lot of my high school experience with queer terminology was getting people to understand them. We did a lot of work with the teachers; we set up safe space programs and things like that.
Religious Life	65% (n = 22)	I definitely went to Keshet [which] is an LGBT Jewish organization that, not only did I go to for resources, I ended up being heavily involved in on a national level and made a lot of friends and went to events with them.
Media	41% (n = 14)	Like everybody who was queer and a teenager in the 2010s, I learned it on Tumblr.
Family & Friends[b]	35% (n = 12)	My [nonbinary] child, they are very aware of not wanting to misgender people, and so anytime someone says, "Oh look, he blah blah blah," my child will say, "Don't assume their gender," so I think that's been really good training for me to just defer to *they*.
Work & Professional Life	29% (n = 10)	I was clueless, but today in [a work] meeting I was asked how I should be referred to, as if they ever mentioned me on Facebook, so I asked to be referred to as *she* and *her*, which is the first time I've been asked this.
Queer History	26% (n = 9)	There is a deep and rich culture of all sorts of different kinds of genders of people within Judaism; it just needs to be discovered and lifted up.
Israel	24% (n = 8)	I always like exploring what are the latest permutations of how Hebrew expresses gender and gender pronouns, especially because pronouns are, like everything, is so gendered in Hebrew, so I am always curious about how Hebrew is developing in Israel and within queer communities that speak Hebrew, how they're dealing with that.

a. EDUCATIONAL SETTINGS that are comprehensive, from pre-K through university levels. Religious education, such as Hebrew school and b'nai mitzvah preparation, were counted as religious life.

b. FRIENDS refers to those made later in life (i.e., not made in pre-K through university settings). We excluded friends made in K–16 as to distinguish this from learning that happened in schools or religious communities at those ages. References to K–16 friends were coded as under educational settings.

because it's like something that they have to keep in mind when they're working. I think there's a lot of people who aren't really involved in any way in that stuff, and so when they come across it they're surprised, like, "WHOA! I didn't expect this, I don't know what I'm doing," and then they get all confused about it.

In addition to identifying concrete influences from educational settings, the idea of the university was also sometimes coded as progressive, as in, "I'm in a space where my synagogue is super open. I work for an organization that is significantly stepping into the space and understands the importance and significance of it, [since] I'm on a college campus, right?"

Parents echoed similar sentiments, learning from their childrens' experiences in schools as well as perceiving even their cis-heterosexual children as more "up-to-date" on queer topics. The home and family became an important site of intergenerational transfer. When asked what challenges they have observed to using queer inclusive language in Jewish spaces, one parent responded, "If you consider the house a Jewish space, then I would say my screwing up the pronouns." Parenting also presented a unique opportunity for discussion around gender and sexuality, such as one parent who "initially thought, oh maybe we'll use singular *they* for our child too, but this somehow that didn't feel quite right, and I didn't meet anyone who does that, including queer folks. [...] It's very, very unusual to use nonbinary pronouns for children, even though it seems like that would be a very natural space to do it."

For many children, Hebrew school and b'nai mitzvah preparation introduced conversations around gender and sexuality in Judaism and Hebrew. One parent recalls asking her nonbinary child

What are you going to call this? Is it a bar mitzvah? Is it a bat mitzvah 'cause biologically and dadada, and they actually said we can call it a bar mitzvah. [...] And here's the irony—you'll love this—[we] got the Torah portion, and it's got all the rules in it about sex, and it's got the part about "a man shall not lie with a man," I was like, "OH MY GOD the ONE LINE IN THE ENTIRE TORAH, boom, we hit it, so I was like "Okay, what are we gonna do with that?" and I figured it'll make a great *dvar Torah* [דבר תורה 'lit. a word of Torah; talk reflecting on that week's Torah portion'].

Media also contributed significantly to queer knowledge, although specific references varied by age. Queer individuals over the age of 30 cited public figures such as Ellen Degeneres and media like *The Rocky Horror Picture Show* (1975), whereas participants generally under the age of 30 cited social media platforms such as Tumblr and TikTok. These online platforms also served as means to learn about queer history that may not otherwise be taught in schools and recent queer language developments being made in Jewish communities worldwide and in colloquial Israeli Hebrew.

ATTITUDES AND FLUENCY IN QUEER JEWISH LANGUAGE ADOPTION. In response to open-ended questions about the terminology that participants use to describe their gender identity and sexual orientation, a number of notable trends arose, particularly stylistic differences between queer and cis-hetero-sexual participants. In response to the question, "If you are comfortable with sharing, how do you describe your gender identity and sexual orientation? What terms do you use?" the 16 cis-heterosexual participants answered with an average of 45 words, in comparison to the 18 queer participants, whose response was over twice as long, with an average of 105 words ($p < .027$). Among queer participants, the 4 who only used *they/them* pronouns averaged 50 words in their responses; the 9 who use only *she/her* or *he/him* pronouns averaged 87 words, and the 5 who used *she/they*, *they/she*, or *he/they* pronouns averaged 181 words. Additionally, participants often used additional descriptors, such as queer identifying folks using terms such as "equal opportunity lover" and "not straight in any way shape or form," and one cishet participant described his identity as "cisgender heterosexual, kind of the classic wonder-bread of gender identities and sexual preferences these days."

Both queer and cis-heterosexual participants brought up their marital status in conjunction with their identities, often linking marriage to the per-formance of sexuality, such as one cishet participant who said she has "been married to the same guy since [year] so I guess that makes me straight." A queer participant stated "I'm a practicing lesbian and my partner, my wife, is a woman." However, marriage discourses often acknowledged intrinsic complexities and contradictions, as in "I am in a heterosexual marriage and so basically identify as heterosexual though in truth I am bisexual. I have had a number of same-sex encounters over the years, though it's been a long time. It's funny, I have a friend who's 27 years into a same-sex relationship but still insist that she be referred to as bisexual."

Of the 16 cishet participants, 8 responded with their pronouns, while only 2 cisgender queer people who exclusively used *he/him* or *she/her* pro-nouns did so. Two cishet participants responded with only their pronouns in lieu of nominal or adjectival descriptors, such as *woman* or *cisgender*. Cishets generally showed greater hesitancy, measured by pauses and dis-course markers, such as one participant who replied "uh *she* and *her* (..) or is it *her* and *she*?"[3] A quarter of cis-heterosexual participants repeated their identity/ies, "straight: and straight and *he/him* (.) does that– (.) is that the right– [grammar]" in comparison to only 2 of the 18 queer participants. Only cis-heterosexual participants listed three pronouns, such as in saying "I use *she her* (..) *hers* pronouns," or coordinated their pronouns with *and*, as in "I use the pronouns *she*: and *her*." In contrast, no queer participants listed three forms of the same pronoun set, and queer participants only listed the two pronouns used without the word *and* (e.g., "I use *they/them* pronouns") with the exception of those using multiple pronoun paradigms, as in "I use *she* and *they* pronouns." Of the 18 queer participants, only 2 cisgender queers and 5 genderqueer participants who used *they/them* pronouns (exclusively or in addition to a second set, out of 9) disclosed their pronouns as means of further elaborating on their identity. One queer participant reflected how

I consider myself a queer, female-bodied individual who is genderqueer, nonbinary in presentation and practice. I use *she/her* and *they/them* pronouns. I'm kind of on a journey with pronouns right now. I like *they/them*, but it does not suit my needs, as I feel kind of out of the gender spectrum in the way we understand it. Societally […] it's not even that I'm outside of it, I just don't agree with it the way that we live it, so why ascribe to it? That's kind of where I am as far as gender. […] This is not a thing that is unified across all peoples and times; it doesn't make a lot of sense to me as far as how we live it here, and I just don't feel part of that gender spectrum in that way, so that's why I use *they/them* and *she/her* interchangeably.

While some felt the inadequacy of *they/them* pronouns, many opted to use it over neopronouns due to the familiarity and general public knowledge of it.

In analyzing the number and duration of pauses participants had when answering the question about describing their gender and sexual orientations (<1 second = short; $1–2$ seconds = medium; >2 seconds = long), notable differences arose among the 16 cis-heterosexual and 18 queer participants ($p = .025$; cishet $s^2 = 5$; queer $s^2 = 40.8$) (see figure 2), and within queer participants that utilize different pronouns ($p < .043$; *she* or *he* pronouns $s^2 = 20.8$; *she/they* and *he/they* $s^2 = 70.92$; *they/them* $s^2 = 1.3$) (see figure 3). The notable absence of long pauses among the 4 users of exclusively *they/them* pronouns may suggest extensive previous thought on the subject that resulted in greater verbal fluency. In contrast, the 5 users of *she/they* and *he/they* pronouns demonstrated more frequent medium and long pauses indicative of "looking for words" to describe their identities, which often corresponded with description of extant language as insufficient, as in:

Yeah: I um I use uh *he* and *THEY* pronouns um: <the *THEY* thing came about relatively recently> after some soul searching 'cause UM I kind of– ended up like not realizing, like (.) <I just don't identify> (..) with GENDER period hhh like I just don't (.) necessarily I don't have like strong feelings about (...) like– (..) anyany gender and I felt like *they/them* refle:cted that a little bit more? um: for me but um (..) yeah I don't know, it's still– it's all a journey: um right now uh I– I definitely like I identify as like <male presenting:> um: (..) and as like a GAY man? m– (..) as GAY >maybe not as a– like I don't know< it's– the gender thing is like– (..) not as: IMPORTANT to me. [unedited]

FIGURE 2

Differences in Pause Distribution between Cis-heterosexual and Queer Participants

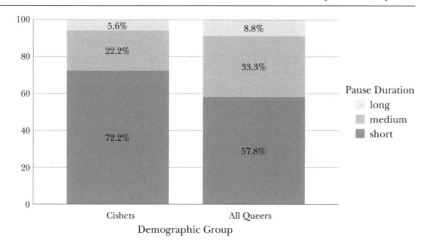

FIGURE 3

Differences in Pause Distribution among Queer Participants
Who Use Different Pronouns

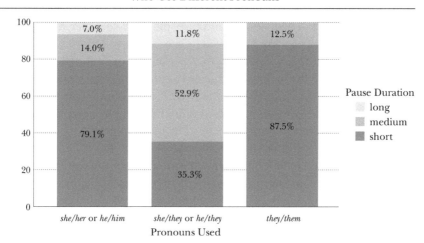

Queer participants also navigated code-switching with two primary approaches. The first is by simplifying language when around cishets who may not be as well educated on queer language, such as one participant who describes how "my sexual identity is panromantic demisexual but to the layperson, I will say I'm bisexual because that is generally easier [...] for people who don't quite know LGBTQ+ things to understand." The second approach focuses on how it is generally better understood in queer communities that identity can be fluid, thus another participant reflects on

When I'm in a queer group, then I'll just kind of be like "eh yeah yeah" [to describe their gender identity] whereas when I'm in a majority cisgender heterosexual group, I'm much more likely to define my identities more specifically because I know that, in general, cis people are less likely to be open to the idea of just "kinda meh […]." When I'm in more cisgender groups or heterosexual groups, I'll probably be more likely to say I'm nonbinary, I'm trans masc.

Queer participants were asked what term they preferred the interviewers use to refer collectively to the LGBTQ+ community, such as *queer community*, *LGBT community*, *LGBTQ+ community*, or any other terms. All said that they preferred *queer* or used *queer* themselves or that they did not care ("whatever is fine"),[4] although some acknowledged that its use was still contentious. Both queer and cis-heterosexual participants described the umbrella term *queer* as both less complicated and more inclusive than *LGBT* or *LGBTQ+*. One queer participant explained that she tends "to use *queer* these days more than I use *lesbian* because *lesbian*'s too granular and sets up barriers because the queer community's gotten a whole lot more diverse, [and] *queer*'s a whole lot easier than the acronym [because it] just got too damn long." A cis-heterosexual participant said, "I actually don't think people even consider what they're always saying when they say *LGTP– LG–* See, all those letters. […] I don't even think they always even know honestly what they're referring to."

Hesitation and disfluency with queer language, described narratively or marked in speech errors, such as in the "LGTP" quote, were common for cis-heterosexual (and to a lesser extent, cisgender LGB) participants. However, both self-cited reasons underlying hesitation and responses to it were varied. Most commonly, individuals lacked or perceived that they lacked fluency in using queer language, due to insufficient practice or exposure, and often cited how rapidly queer language evolves and the perceived difficulty of "keeping up" (Burridge and Benczes 2019; Dy and Perleberg 2021). Several cisgender participants also described discomfort making mistakes or "using the wrong words" as an obstacle to language advocacy and allyship. This attitude contrasts with several genderqueer participants' statements that inclusive and affirming language was simple, and something one "just did," as in:

If you know whatever pronouns or terms that someone identifies as that's what I'm going to use. […] I think, I really think, it's as simple as that. Whatever language I'm learning or whatever language I'm speaking, you know, if someone wants to be addressed or talked about a certain way, then that's how I'm going to talk about them, regardless of if it's about gender or sexuality or whatever other type of identity. […] I'm gonna go with what my friend wants me to use.

Some participants were concerned that having opinions on queer language as a cis-heterosexual or on trans/genderqueer language as a cisgender person was overstepping, as in "I think I'm the wrong person to ask that question?"

DIRECTIONS FOR FURTHERING QUEER INCLUSION. In the words of one partici-pant, "Seattle is a place where we think we're really liberal and wonderful, but then when you drill down just one layer, you start to see that there's a lot of talk and not a lot of do." One queer participant emphasized the discrep-ancy between knowledge and practice of queer inclusion, describing "smart responsible academics in the humanities [who] had read about queer issues, and cognitively knew about it, but as far as making those choices directly, it didn't always manifest."

The relational dynamic of this learning reemphasizes the limited impact of queer affirming material symbols relative to hiring and retaining queer individuals. The importance of hiring and sustained support of diverse clergy and staff is amplified by one queer lay leader, who calls on institutions to reflect on

how we're going to diversify our staffs and how we're going to diversify our voices and how we're going to amplify different voices and center different voices. I mean, I think like that, you know, just that doesn't just happen naturally, so I think there needs to be like real, intentional trainings because that is goes along with our values as Jewish people so it's not even like something we should have to question or think twice about. [...] We should hire consultants that can work us through those changes after we do the training, so that it's not just like, "Oh great, we all feel great about ourselves," but like, "Let's invest in creating a better future for this organization," that takes that into consideration so it can be healthy going forward. That's what I want to see.

When asked about challenges faced in enacting queer inclusive language in Jewish spaces, a queer rabbi jokingly responded with "How long is your time?" indicating the range of challenges queer professionals continue to face. The importance of self-education to reduce intellectual and emotional strains placed on queer individuals, particularly genderqueer and trans people, is critical for cis-heterosexual allies, notably those in clerical roles who were frequently cited as influential educators in the Seattle Jewish community. One rabbi remarked how

I would love for our greater Jewish organizations to really try to include more model-ing [of] queer language and modeling, that June is not the only time to be queer, and that there is a deep and rich culture of all sorts of different kinds of genders of people within Judaism, it just needs to be discovered and lifted up. [...] I would like to see all of our institutions mine included be a bit more transparent in that way.

Another queer participant shares their vision of reimagining queerness more expansively, which queer Jewish language facilitates and builds upon.

In general, I would like to see a wider acceptance of what a queer narrative looks like, because I think where I run into a lot of issues as a Jewish queer person is the expectation that "all queer people are atheist," all queer people conform to one societal narrative of like the White flamboyant gay man who speaks in the gay accent, and that is what the gay person is, and that erases religious minorities, that erases racial minorities, that erases basically anyone who didn't have that specific identity and linguistic experience, and that's not what the queer community is at all. I would really like to see the queer community and the general idea of the queer community remember that there is more than one <way to be queer> and accept other expressions into the common vernacular.

LIMITATIONS AND FUTURE RESEARCH. While this study aimed to involve participants from a broad range of roles and perspectives in the Seattle Jewish community, volunteer bias in openness to discuss LGBTQ+ issues through an interview may have shifted the findings to be more affirming than may have been found through an anonymous survey form. IRB restrictions prohibited participation by minors, limiting youth perspectives. Moreover, as the interviews were conducted relatively early in COVID-19 pandemic, future research may better reflect the sociocultural shifts effected by COVID-19 and the opportunity for many to reflect on and reevaluate personal identity as well as longitudinal analysis of individuals' roles in institutional cultural change.

CONCLUSION

This study examines the perception and reality of Seattle progressive identity as it relates to queer Jewish language adoption in Seattle. It finds that, while some cis-heterosexual participants did explicitly rank Seattle and Seattle Jewish communities as leaders in queer inclusion relative to the rest of the nation, most participants drew attention to inconsistencies, systemic failures, and potential areas for growth. Social network analysis illuminates the mechanisms of queer language learning and transfer in Seattle Jewish communities, finding that a small number of trans/genderqueer people, most of whom held leadership roles in Jewish institutions, were regularly cited as sources both of knowledge of queer Jewish language and of the adoption of queer-inclusive language practices in Jewish institutions.

NOTES

We would like to thank our research participants, Kirby Conrod, Abby and Hannah Dy, Ayden Loughlin, Selim Kuru, Michael McAdams, Liz Besser, and the faculty and staff of the University of Washington's Stroum Center for Jewish Studies. With special thanks to Kirby Conrod. Participant quotes are lightly edited for brevity and clarity.

1. Sequim is a small town on the Olympic Peninsula.
2. The Committee on Jewish Law and Standards reviews questions regarding Jewish law for the Conservative movement. The Conservative movement refers to a liturgical tradition, not a political affiliation. The adverb *halakhicly* is dervied from *Halakhah* (הלכה) 'lit. the way; Jewish law'.
3. Transcription conventions used in this article include (.) to represent pauses (with the number of periods indicating relative length), : as a length mark, capitalization for emphasis, and angle brackets for speaking rate.
4. All interviews were conducted by two researchers, at least one of whom was queer, and interviewers' positionality was made explicit to participants upon request. The preference for *queer* may therefore be dependent upon the interlocutor's shared identity for some speakers.

REFERENCES

Balk, Gene. 2020. "More Than 10% of Seattle Residents Identify as LGBTQ+—on Par with San Francisco." *Seattle Times*, Oct. 10, 2020. https://www.seattletimes .com/seattle-news/data/more-than-10-of-seattle-residents-identify-as-lgbtq-on -par-with-san-francisco/.

Barringer, M. N. 2020. "Lesbian, Gay, and Bisexual Individuals' Perceptions of American Religious Traditions." *Journal of Homosexuality* 67, no. 9: 1173–96. https://doi.org/10.1080/00918369.2019.1582221.

Battistella, Ed, Kristin Denham, and Anne Lobeck. 2020. "Pacific Voices, 2014–2019." Progress report posted on *Literary Ashland* (blog) by Ed Battistella, Jan. 1, 2021. https://literaryashland.org/?p=11499.

Benor, Sarah Bunin. 2009. "Do American Jews Speak a 'Jewish Language'? A Model of Jewish Linguistic Distinctiveness." *Jewish Quarterly Review* 99, no. 2 (Spring): 230–69. https://doi.org/10.1353/jqr.0.0046.

Boxer, Matthew, Janet Krasner Aronson, Matthew A. Brown, and Leonard Saxe. 2015. "2014 Greater Seattle Jewish Community Study." Cohen Center for Modern Jewish Studies, the Steinhardt Social Research Institute at Brandeis University, and the Jewish Federation of Greater Seattle. https://www.brandeis.edu/cmjs/ community-studies/seattle-report.html.

Brennan-Ing, Mark, Liz Seidel, Britta Larson, and Stephen E Karpiak. 2013. "'I'm Created in God's Image, and God Don't Create Junk': Religious Participation and Support among Older GLBT Adults." *Journal of Religion, Spirituality, and Aging* 25, no. 2: 70–92. https://doi.org/10.1080/15528030.2013.746629.

Bronfenbrenner, Urie. 1995. "Developmental Ecology through Space and Time: A Future Perspective." In *Examining Lives in Context: Perspectives on the Ecology of Human Development*, edited by Phyllis Moen, Glenn H. Elder, Jr., and Kurt Lüscher, 619–47. Washington, D.C.: American Psychological Association.

Bucholtz, Mary, and Kira Hall. 2005. "Identity and Interaction: A Sociocultural Linguistic Approach." *Discourse Studies* 7, nos. 4–5 (Oct.): 585–614. https://doi.org/10.1177/1461445605054407.

Burridge, Kate, and Réka Benczes. 2019. "Taboo as a Driver of Language Change." In *The Oxford Handbook of Taboo Words and Language*, edited by Keith Allan, 180–98. Oxford: Oxford University Press.

Conrod, Kirby. 2019. "Pronouns Raising and Emerging." Ph.D. diss., University of Washington.

Crenshaw, Kimberle. 1987. "Demarginalizing the Intersection of Race and Sex: A Black Feminist Critique of Antidiscrimination Doctrine, Feminist Theory and Antiracist Politics." *University of Chicago Legal Forum* 1987, art. 8. https://chicago unbound.uchicago.edu/uclf/vol1989/iss1/8.

Dy, Grace Elizabeth, and Ellen Perleberg. 2021. "'We've Been Through Worse': The Impacts of COVID-19 on LGBTQ+ Jewish Language in Seattle." *I-LanD Journal: Identity, Language and Diversity* 2021, no. 2: 68–91. https://doi.org/10.26379/IL2021002_005.

FitzMorris, Mary K. 2014. "The Last Generation of Native Ladino Speakers? Judeo-Spanish and the Sephardic Community in Seattle." M.A. thesis, University of Washington.

Gregory, James N. 2015. "Seattle's Left Coast Formula." *Dissent* 62, no. 1 (Winter): 64–70. https://doi.org/10.1353/dss.2015.0012.

Gross, Lior, and Eyal Rivlin. 2021. Nonbinary Hebrew Project. https://www.non binaryhebrew.com/.

Human Rights Campaign. 2015. "Stances of Faiths on LGBTQ+ Issues: Reform Judaism." HRC Foundation. Nov. 19, 2015. https://www.hrc.org/resources/stances -of-faiths-on-lgbt-issues-reform-judaism.

Levon, Erez. 2015. "Integrating Intersectionality in Language, Gender, and Sexuality Research." *Language and Linguistics Compass* 9 no. 7 (June): 295–308. https://doi.org/10.1111/lnc3.12147.

Loughlin, Ayden. 2021. "Frequency of Singular *they* for Gender Stereotypes and the Influence of the Queer Community." Paper presented at the 27th Annual Lavender Languages and Linguistics Conference, May 21–23, 2021, virtual.

Kukla, Elliot. 2006. "Terms for Gender Diversity in Classical Jewish Texts." *Trans Torah*, 2006. http://www.transtorah.org/PDFs/Classical_Jewish_Terms_for _Gender_Diversity.pdf.

Maxwell, Nancy Kalikow. 2019. *Typically Jewish*. Lincoln: University of Nebraska Press.

McKenna, Kevin, and Michael Aguirre. 2016. "A Brief History of LGBTQ Activism in Seattle." The Seattle Civil Rights and Labor History Project, University of Washington. https://depts.washington.edu/civilr/lgbtq_history.htm.

Milgram, Stanley. 1967. "The Small-World Problem." *Psychology Today* 1, no. 1 (May): 61–67.

Milroy, Lesley. 1987. *Language and Social Networks.* 2nd ed. Oxford: Blackwell.

Milton, Cole. 2020. "The Buffering Effect of Chosen Family Networks in LGBT Adults." M.A. thesis, Southern Illinois University at Carbondale.

Perleberg, Ellen, and Grace Elizabeth Dy. 2022. "Growing Up on the Wrong Side of the *Mechitza*: A Case Study of Contemporary Queer Jewish Language." *Journal of Jewish Languages* 10, no. 1: 120–39. https://doi.org/10.1163/22134638-bja10019.

Pew Research Center. 2013. "A Portrait of Jewish Americans: Findings from the Pew Research Center Survey of U.S. Jews." Pew Research Center's Religion and Public Life Project, Oct. 1, 2013. https://www.pewforum.org/2013/10/01/jewish-american-beliefs-attitudes-culture-survey/.

Pew Research Center. 2021. "Jewish Americans in 2020: U.S. Jews Are Culturally Engaged, Increasingly Diverse, Politically Polarized and Worried abou Anti-Semitism." May 11, 2021. https://www.pewforum.org/2021/05/11/jewish-americans-in-2020/.

Raghavendran, Beena. 2015. "Colorful Crosswalks Celebrate Gay Pride in Seattle." *Seattle Times,* June 23, 2015. https://www.seattletimes.com/seattle-news/colorful-crosswalks-celebrate-gay-pride-in-seattle/.

Renkert, Lauren Ella. 2005. "From Father to Child: An Application of the Process-Person-Context-Time Model." Ph.D. diss., University of Tennessee, Knoxville.

Shoemaker, Pamela J., and Tim P. Vos. 2009. *Gatekeeping Theory.* New York: Routledge.

Smorag, Pascale. 2008. "From Closet Talk to PC Terminology : Gay Speech and the Politics of Visibility." *Transatlantica* 2008, no. 1: art. 3503. Association Française d'Etudes Américaines. https://doi.org/10.4000/transatlantica.3503.

Wassink, Alicia Beckford. 2015. "Sociolinguistic Patterns in Seattle English." *Language Variation and Change* 27, no. 1 (Mar.): 31–58. https://doi.org/10.1017/S0954394514000234.

Wolowic, Jennifer M., Laura V. Heston, Elizabeth M. Saewyc, Carolyn Porta, and Marla E. Eisenberg. 2017. "Chasing the Rainbow: Lesbian, Gay, Bisexual, Transgender and Queer Youth and Pride Semiotics." *Culture, Health and Sexuality* 19, no. 5: 557–71. https://doi.org/10.1080/13691058.2016.1251613.

ELLEN PERLEBERG is a master of science in library science student at the University of North Carolina at Chapel Hill and the coprincipal investigator of the Yallah Y'all queer Jewish sociolinguistics project at the University of Washington. Her research interests include heritage language learners, digital language, and labor discourse. Email: eperly@uw.edu.

GRACE ELIZABETH C. DY is the coprincipal investigator of Yallah Y'all and is the events and outreach coordinator at the Stroum Center for Jewish Studies at the University of Washington. They are also a graduate student in counseling psychology, with research interests in culturally responsive mental health, equitable teaching practices, and the intersection of science and religion. Email: dyg@uw.edu.

LINDSAY HIPPE is a fourth-year undergraduate student at the University of Washington pursuing a double degree in linguistics and in speech and hearing sciences. Her research interests include Semitic languages and early childhood language acquisition. She hopes to become a research speech-language pathologist with a focus on early support. Email: lhippe@uw.edu.

ROOT ROT: LINGUISTIC CONFLICTS OF PLACE AND AGENCY

TYLER KIBBEY

Humboldt-Universität zu Berlin

ABSTRACT: This article presents a counter-theoretical commentary on Paul Reed's rootedness as an epistemological framework for quantifying the measurement and linguistic realization of place attachment. By examining researcher positionality and problematizing rootedness when examining implications for the study of queer communities, the author shows how the current rootedness framework fails to adequately account for social conflicts between place and agency. Moreover, the author presents a theoretical expansion or counter-theory complementing Reed's rootedness notion rather than criticizing it. The author explores how personal evaluations of security and communal hostility might undermine current metrics for the study of rootedness in these populations and outline (UP)ROOTEDNESS and ROOT ROT as a means of accounting for these complexities.

KEYWORDS: region, sexuality, gender, violence, identity

WHEN I DIE, PLANT ME ON THE RIDGE." Standing on a hill overlooking the fields of the family farm, this was the only time I heard my grandfather mention his own mortality. It was only after he died, when we cleaned up an old cemetery on that same ridge, where long ago some family known by the name of Brown had laid their own loved ones to rest, and only when we lowered his casket into the ground, that the peculiarity of his request struck me. At what is now the Kibbey-Brown Cemetery, my family has put down permanent roots in Tennessee for the first time.

Now I mention this to highlight the powerful affective nature of rootedness as both a formal epistemological frame and as a folk theory of place attachment. Reed (2016) first operationalizes rootedness in the study of /aɪ/ monopthongization and rising pitch accents in East Tennessee, showcasing how the cognitive reality of place influences the realization of variable linguistic forms:

Rootedness, a speaker's connection to place, appears to influence and to impact various aspects of a speaker's linguistic production. All too often, region is considered to be a categorical factor in sociolinguistic investigations. All speakers from a particular locale are lumped together, e.g., Southerners, Californians, etc. However, such practices will miss the crucial and far-reaching impact of how a speaker relates to place. It is not merely where a speaker is from, rather how a speaker relates to place. [Reed 2020b, 112]

American Speech, Vol. 98, No. 1, February 2023   DOI 10.1215/00031283-10579481

I cannot help but intuitively agree that the longer we stay in one place—the longer our family stays in one place—the more strongly we become tethered to what is otherwise a rather unremarkable point on a map. Our memories and experiences of a particular place as well as our relationship with the people there ground us in that space just as roots fasten a tree to the earth. Elsewhere we might intentionally "put down roots," or in the wake of misfortune we might be "uprooted" suddenly. And this is to say nothing of related plant metaphors for family and familial relationships (e.g., *family tree*, *the apple doesn't fall far from the tree*, etc.). Rootedness speaks to the relationship between individual and place in ways that many formal, overly theorized frameworks cannot. Needless to say, I am a great admirer of Reed's work on rootedness (e.g., Reed 2016, 2018, 2020a). It is an exciting framework, both from a theoretical and a methodological perspective, and should I ever wish to study linguistic variation as it is related to place attachment in an exclusively cisgender and heterosexual population, rootedness will be my starting point for such a project. However, as compelling as I find this epistemological framework, it betrays startling gaps in the field of dialectology and sociolinguistics with respect to identity, positionality, and diversity. It also provides a rather unique opportunity to address these gaps.

Paul Reed and I are both from the northern border of Tennessee, come from a similar socioeconomic background, and have had similar cultural experiences. We were in fact raised only a handful of counties apart: Hancock County and Sumner County, respectively. Intuitively, I expect that our shared experiences in this regard lead us to find rootedness compelling for similar reasons. However, whereas I am a queer, nonbinary linguist, Reed is not. It is within this conceptual frame that I consider and comment upon Reed's conception of ROOTEDNESS as a dialectological metric for place attachment (2016, 2020a). I argue in the following sections that it is crucial for the development of our science—and specifically the study of language, place, and identity—to question tacit epistemologies and positionalities as they appear in the implicit subjectivity of research and conversely to engage in explicit counter-theorization of those epistemologies. While some may see this as a bad faith critique of Reed's theorization of rootedness, I again invite the reader to engage with the present work as an expansion of theory rather than a reduction. If rootedness can explicate the nuanced relationship between place and language, what then might we learn from uprooted language communities and speakers, those whose "roots are left to rot" either as a result of neglect or directed acts of violence, and those who have little to no say in where they are permitted to "put down roots." In this commentary, I seek to address the latter through a critique of the former and showcase how linguistic science is enriched by the occasional consideration of positionality in theory, a fact well known but not well studied.

ROOTEDNESS AS EPISTEMOLOGY

Linguistics is unique among the sciences in an historiographical sense, being caught between the natural sciences, the social sciences, and the humanities. Historically, both in the development of its theories and its methodologies, linguistics has rightly—to a certain extent—tended toward a greater affinity with the natural sciences and, to a lesser extent, the social sciences. This has placed an emphasis on the primacy of the research object within the modern discipline of linguistic science, near-completely effacing the subject of research (i.e., researcher) as anything more than a statistically troubling observer. Language as an object is held to be independent of the linguist as subject, and the social realities that shape language are similarly held to be separate and distinct from the researcher, belonging instead to the non-expert language-using population. At least, this is true of the discipline in a formalist sense, though there does exist a body of transdisciplinary work within American dialectology that does seek to bridge these gaps (see, e.g., Wolfram and Schilling-Estes 1998, 263–344; Wolfram 2015; see Childs 2021; Kibbey 2019, 2021 for discussion of transdisciplinarity). There have also been extensive recent critiques of the problems that arise from these implicit biases in the literature outside of what might be called a philosophy of linguistics (Dobrin and Good 2009; Baugh 2018; Charity Hudley, Mallinson, and Bucholtz 2020). However, similar problems with gender and sexuality as variables in linguistic research, in relation to LGBTQ+ and non-LGBTQ+ language usage, are often perceived as less obvious (for discussion, see Leap and Boellstorff 2004; Zimman, Davis, and Raclaw 2014; Barrett 2017) or not treated as necessarily imperative.

What has struck me with Reed's program of research is that, even though rootedness as a metric of place-attachment is intriguing both in its operationalization and in its objective design, rootedness as an epistemological framework takes for granted several implicit assumptions about the social reality of place in relation to gender and sexuality. Reed (2020a) gives his Rootedness Metric survey categories as (1) willingness to relocate, (2) travel habits, (3) where a participant claims to be from, (4) family history, (5) areal identification, (6) how much they participate in local events, and (7) self-reported strength of local identity. Of these seven categories, willingness to relocate, travel habits, how much they participate in local events, and self-reported local identity are all likely to be affected by the dynamic and often complex social reality of existing as a gender and/or sexual minority in relation to a specific place. For queer and trans individuals, willingness to relocate is affected by the danger of anti-LGBTQ+ violence in one place compared to the presence of civil rights guarantees in other places. A recent example is the institution of antitrans legislation in a number of states that have effectively criminalized the existence of trans children. Laws that criminalize gender affirming care for transgender youth then force individuals and families to choose between the place they live, possibly where their family has lived for generations, and the personal well-being of trans children. The threat of violence is also a pressing issue within families, with youth homelessness and housing instability disproportionately affecting LGBTQ+ adolescents who either run away from home or are kicked out of their homes because of their gender or sexuality and how such identities conflict with the theo-political ideologies of their parents (DeChants et al. 2021). In the words of mid-century queer essayist Merle Miller (2071, 28), "Naturally. If you were *that way*, what else could you expect? Either they ran you out of town or you left before they got around to it." Similarly, travel habits can be affected by these pressures in a primary or secondary sense: LGBTQ+ individuals are less likely to leave affirming places for less-affirming places and are more likely to leave less-affirming places for affirming places, with these behaviors being facilitated by broad evaluations of personal risk. Evaluations of personal risk as well as a general absence of civil rights protections also mitigate the abil-ity of queer and trans people to participate in local events in certain states and regions, which combined with the pressures related to travel habits, mentioned above, may also affect areal identification and where a person claims to be from.

Broadly speaking, rootedness and conventional epistemologies of place in American dialectology can accommodate queer experiences of place and place attachment, but such accommodation is a secondary impulse. A robust sociolinguistic theory of place attachment must account for social complex-ity and not simply accommodate it as an afterthought. More than anything, this represents the underlying theoretical impulse of the present article: while rootedness can be applied to the study of LGBTQ+ populations, with some adjustments, it should not be done so offhandedly or without suitable counter-theorizing.

Rootedness is not the only epistemological framework for place (attach-ment) in dialectology and sociolinguistics, however. Rather, rootedness in many ways represents the logical end point of a tradition that has been slowly moving away from treating place as a categorical factor in the study of language. Borderlands have become a central element in complicating con-temporary dialectological ideas of place. Cramer's (2016) study of language usage and ideology in Louisville, Kentucky—a border city that straddles the Ohio River on the Kentucky-Indiana border—is one such example. Empha-sizing how linguistic variation in border regions exemplifies the fluidity of regional identity at regional, cultural, dialectal, and geographical borders,

Cramer argues that "borderlands appear to be important locations for the examination of identity, specifically as it relates to language perception and use" (164). Other work in dialectology and complex systems theory has also shown that many of our constructed dialectal borders (i.e., isoglosses) are more porous than we had otherwise expected, with nonlinear relationships between variables affecting distribution as part of a much larger system (Kretzschmar 2015; Burkette and Kretzschmar 2018).

THE LIMINALITY AND POSITIONALITY
OF QUEER EXPERIENCE

Queerness, as an inherently nonnormative experience, occupies liminal spaces, both literally and figuratively. Liminality designates transitional spaces (hence the use of *trans*), such as provided by the imagery of doorways, train platforms, and bus stops through which people pass when moving from one place to another. When discussing queer experience, however, liminality also refers to the peripheralization of queer bodies in the wider sociopolitical system that surrounds them. Reminiscent of Sedgwick's (2008) deconstruction of the proverbial closet, liminality is a negotiation of identities and normative ideologies that have been forced into opposition. Pushed to the outermost borders of polite society, never secure in our rights, our civil liberties, forced to negotiate constantly between normative and nonnormative expression as a matter of self-preservation, queer liminality is an expression of the ephemeral, the transitional, and all things hidden just out of sight.

While not always referred to as liminality, the peripheral and transitional experiences that are all but universal to queerness are a common theme within the literature of multiple disciplines. Boswell's (1980, 1994) detailed history of homosexuality in Medieval Europe frequently emphasizes the boundary between urban and rural spaces, especially how urban-rural demographic changes influenced ideologies of sexual morality; and more recently, Manion's (2020) trans history of female husbands in the United States and United Kingdom prior to the twentieth century highlights the struggle of nonnormative identity at the crossroads of political, social, and economic hierarchies, each infused with its own particular expression of gender ideology within place-sensitive contexts. Within literature on the psychology of gender, Fausto-Sterling (2000) discusses how notions of sex and gender binaries force intersex individuals into a medically untenable position (from the point of view of cisgender medical professionals) that often results in "corrective" surgery in early childhood. From a sociological perspective, Ward (2015) discusses how some straight White men have sex with other straight White men as a way of reinforcing heterosexuality and masculinity, indicating an existing fluidity of experience even among those with cis-heteronormative identities. In queer feminist philosophy, Butler (1990) and Sedgwick (2008) both discuss how essentialist binaries break-down in the context of queer identity and experience; and Anzaldúa (1999) details the marginalizing forces of queerness at the intersection of minority ethnic, racial, and linguistic identities within the mestiza and tejana cultures at the U.S.-Mexico border. She writes, for example, "as a *mestiza* I have no country, my homeland cast me out; yet all countries are mine because I am every woman's sister or potential lover. (As a lesbian I have no race, my own people disclaim me; but I am all races because there is the queer of me in all races.)" (86). While the term is rarely used, the central notion of liminal-ity—transitions, peripherality, placelessness—can be seen to unify much of the writing on queer issues in numerous disciplines.

Within the discipline of linguistics, the use of language to negotiate and index identity within liminal spaces is well documented. Early queer linguistic research tended to focus on the lexicogrammatical elements of "codes" used as a means of communication between queer people in times and places where nonnormative gender and sexual identities were considered criminal by the state (see Barrett 2006; Queen 2007). The earliest example of this impulse may be observed in Legman's (1941) glossary of homosexual slang, which included "words and phrases current in American slang, argot, and colloquial speech since the First World War" commonly used by gay men in the 1930s (19). Contemporary studies in queer language, however, largely reject such reductive ideas regarding the relationship between language, gen-der, and sexuality. Barrett (2017) further demonstrates that queer liminality and queer language do not constitute a unitary indexical system; instead, he shows how language used to index queer identity is complicated by race, ethnicity, and class, structuring linguistic counter-cultures within counter-cultures. Surveying language usage among African American drag queens, for example, he argues that "white-woman" style speech is "typically used to create indexical polysemy through dialect opposition [with AAE, which] is used to create specific personas and shifting identities throughout the course of the performance, often interrogating hegemonic assumptions about race and class" (48). Levon (2014) shows how pitch variation in queer spaces is influenced by both conversational frames and subjective conceptualizations of belonging within the complex sociopolitical economy of modern Israel. And McCleary's (2023 [this issue]) analysis of community language among drag performers in Oklahoma City demonstrates how the negotiation of liminal spaces and regional identity are structured at various levels of locality within the queer 39th Street enclave of Oklahoma City.

ROOT ROT, CONFLICTS OF PLACE AND AGENCY

Now, how queer scholars position their own experiences within the broader study of a particular subject is another matter entirely. The double-edged blade of queer academia has widely been discussed by queer, and more recently trans, scholars (Halperin 1995): the contradiction that even the most objective science or incidental philosophy is necessarily queer by association and the expectation that the queer scholar stands as monolith for all queer experience within a particular discipline. Counter-theorizing has long served a central function in the queering of disciplinary projects. Halberstam (2011) differentiates between high theory and low theory to demonstrate how antidisciplinary work problematizes the high-brow projects of the university and its inherent, peripheralizing effects on minority scholars. Counter-theorizing, in this sense, does not necessitate disagreement, nor does it require discipline to legitimize its position. Rather, counter-theorizing radically centers on the experiences of the researcher in their approach to theory and its application, linking it inextricably to what we might call positionality. Now, this is not to say that engagement with positionality is in any way absent from Reed's (2016, 2020b) work on rootedness. In fact, he makes it very clear that his lived experiences and identity are central in his approach to selecting a particular population to study and in how he develops a theory to describe how they use language. He writes, for example, "I focus on Appalachia because of this clear sense of place, this cognitive reality of the importance of place, and because it is meaningful to me as a native to the region" (2020b, 107). In its own right, Reed's writing on place attachment in Appalachia is counter-theoretical in its resistance to prevailing conceptualizations of Appalachia, dialect boundaries, and socioeconomic influences on place attachment. However, like much of the work in linguistics that is decidedly not queer, rootedness possesses an undercurrent of would-be-generalization that, if left unaddressed, would exclude the queer subject from this exciting new area of research.

Returning now, here at the end, to the issue of rootedness as an epistemological framework, I would ask the reader to consider what it means to be uprooted from a particular place, especially with reference to my above discussion of queer liminality. In preparing this article, I chose the title "root rot" to specifically highlight how a hostile environment can affect rootedness. Uprootedness implies an external agent that may not be specific to a particular location. People can be uprooted by war, famine, and natural disasters; intentionally moved to make way for state-backed projects; or increasingly, displaced by the effects of climate change. Certain classes of individuals might be forced to move from their home or relocated to some far away place either because of interpersonal pressures (e.g., the elderly, people with disabilities, those institutionalized by the state or family members, prisoners). There may also be legal restrictions or threats of violence, implied or otherwise, that limit movement for members of minority ethnic, racial, or religious groups, such as was the case in the Jim Crow era and can still be observed in the intergenerational effects segregation has had on African American language communities (e.g., see Grieser 2022). In this sense, uprootedness is not the opposite of rootedness: while the latter concerns an individual's relation to place, the former conveys a sense of how others limit an individual's ability to relate to place.

Root rot, on the other hand, returns agency to the individual and how a particular place affects that person's relation to it. In a literal sense, root rot is a condition where roots begin to mold and rot in overly saturated soil over varying periods of time. The environment becomes unsuitable for the plant and will eventually cause it to wither and die. Different species of plant have different tolerances and environmental optimality, but the effect is the same. Despite every impulse of nature to the contrary, it is no longer rooted securely in the earth and the rot spreads to the rest of the plant. In an analogical sense, measuring rootedness in queer populations may paradoxically show both strong and weak rootedness scores dependent upon the place-attachment variables being measured, the relative hostility of the local community to LGBTQ+ identities, and the personal security of a particular individual. When I first read Reed's work on rootedness (2016, and elsewhere), there was a moment of recognition, an "Oh, that's why I do that" moment, where a facet of my use of language to relate to my home in Tennessee was made suddenly clear. This moment of recognition, however, was immediately followed by a prevailing confusion, that by all accounts this theory indicates I should have incredibly weak rootedness and likewise should be speaking in a manner consistent with a middling degree of place attachment. The contradiction of strong place attachment in an incredibly hostile environment, while not unheard of, was left unaccounted for within the growing literature on rootedness.

A few examples of such a relationship may be observed in places of forced, involuntary relocation (refugee camps, prisons, nursing homes, etc.) as well as in diasporic contexts (large-scale population movement in transnational spaces). With respect to the latter, there is a growing body of literature that supports the argument that minority gender identities and sexualities are doubly vulnerable in these spaces, as queer(ed) bodies are forced to navigate mutually reinforcing ideologies of social, racial, and religious exclusion (see Luibhéid and Chávez 2020; Hernández, Alvarez, and García 2021; van Klinken et al. 2021).

What I have argued here is that, while it is possible to understand the relationship between place, identity, and language without reference to agency, it is a grave oversight to do so. Even if unintentional, it can create a theoretical gap in the study of how marginalized communities use language to relate to place that can then only grow in magnitude until any attempt at counter-theorizing is no longer complementary but contradictory. At the same time the sociopolitical pressures underlying queer liminality, as might be observed in the linguistic realization of regional identity, are not unique to queer and trans communities but might also be observed, as stated previously, in other marginalized communities. The Chicano culture of the southwestern United States is a clear example. In the 1848 Treaty of Guadalupe Hidalgo, which ended the Mexican-American War, Mexico ceded a majority of its northern territory to the United States and overnight Mexican citizens became American citizens. In her chapter on the wild tongues of the borderlands, Anzaldúa (1999, 85) details how negotiating between Spanish, English, and the regional dialects of each reflects not only how she identifies with place but how she reifies her identity and in what contexts:

When not copping out, when we know we are more than nothing, we call ourselves Mexican, referring to race and ancestry; *mestizo* when affirming both our Indian and Spanish (but we hardly ever own our Black ancestry); Chicano when referring to a politically aware people born and/or raised in the U.S.; *Raza* when referring to Chicanos; *tejanos* when we are Chicanos from Texas.

And this is to say nothing of how sexuality and gender complicate these already complex relationships, as she discusses elsewhere. If there can be counter-cultures within counter-cultures and counter-theories within counter-theories, then surely there are also liminal spaces within liminal spaces, as well as roots willing to grow there.

CONCLUSION

Like many queer and trans individuals, my childhood experience of home is defined by the constant tension between safety, violence, closetedness, and the self. Throughout my grade school years, even till today, a Bible quote attributed to a purportedly omnibenevolent deity stood out on a billboard aside the road into town: "You shall not lie with a man as with a woman. It is an abomination. –God." During my sophomore year of high school, one of only three openly gay classmates was gang-raped during school hours. That year one of the others was badly beaten walking home from school. The next year I decided to graduate early so I could flee my home for the university, only to find the state legislature engaged in a war of attrition against the University of Tennessee's LGBTQ+ community (Kibbey, forthcoming). The following year, my hometown outlawed "adult performances" within one mile of any church in city limits, effectively shuttering a weekly drag show that had been quietly held on the town's periphery for well over a decade. Few of my fellow queer and trans classmates have stayed, and those who remain are forced to the town's cultural and sociopolitical periphery.

Yet, despite this, I possess a strong sense of rootedness with respect to my home, and this is reflected linguistically and discursively in many different contexts. A small part of me still dreams of one day returning to the family farm to set up shop and put down roots of my own, spending what little time I have enjoying the hills and hollers of Tennessee. Raising cattle, hunting deer, fishing in the creek, and perhaps every other cliché as well, if I have the time—this is a dream of a home denied by communal, sociopolitical threats of violence, implicit and explicit, in the cultural climate of the Tennessee-Kentucky border. While I assert the importance of positionality in the development of theory, especially in the charged political climate of the contemporary United States, I cannot completely dismiss that things are changing—not always for the better, but changing nonetheless. After I graduated college, I visited home to see my brothers—the only reason I go home anymore. I decided it was time to come out to my youngest brother so that he could understand why our family treated me differently. I sat him down and explained things, emphasizing that queer and trans experience was a natural part of life, to which he replied, "Yeah, I don't care. I have trans friends. It's cool," in the undercutting, blasé tone that only a middle-schooler can produce.

That being said, root rot still characterizes the majority of queer experiences with place and place attachment and will likely continue to do so for at least another generation in the United States. At the intersection of other marginalized identities—racial, ethnic, disability, socioeconomic, and so on—root rot will likely characterize experiences of place attachment for many generations to come. Now, to address the obvious, this article is not data driven. It engages with theory and only theory; though counter-theoretical, it offers no counter-data-points. My principal program of research focuses on the relationship between religion, cognition, and violence as it is negotiated linguistically to oppress, marginalize, and disenfranchise queer and trans peoples around the world. Given what I have shared of my own personal experiences, I am sure the reader can understand why this is my principal area of study. As such, my work is more focused on the causes of root rot rather than their effects in the language of LGBTQ+ communities, in the same way that a chemist and a toxicologist both do and do not study the same thing. To this end, I have crafted an essay that operationalizes, at least to some degree, work on the study of violence to the benefit of a queer and trans dialectology and a general theory of rootedness that accommodates, from the outset, a greater diversity of human experience. My hope, as is the hope inherent to the present issue, is that a greater understanding of the relationship between gender, sexuality, and regional identity as expressed through language might yet help us to better understand each other and in so doing might allow those who wish the freedom to return to their roots.

REFERENCES

Anzaldúa, Gloria. 1999. *Borderlands = La Frontera: The New Mestiza.* 2nd ed. San Francisco, Calif.: Aunt Lute Books.

Barrett, Rusty. 2006. "Queer Talk." In *Encyclopedia of Language and Linguistics,* 2nd ed., edited by Keith Brown, 10: 316–22. Boston: Elsevier.

Barrett, Rusty. 2017. *From Drag Queens to Leathermen: Language, Gender, and Gay Male Subculture.* New York: Oxford University Press.

Baugh, John. 2018. *Linguistics in Pursuit of Justice.* Cambridge: Cambridge University Press.

Boswell, John. 1980. *Christianity, Social Tolerance, and Homosexuality: Gay People in Western Europe from the Beginning of the Christian Era to the Fourteenth Century.* Chicago: University of Chicago Press.

Boswell, John. 1994. *Same-Sex Unions in Premodern Europe.* New York: Villard Books.

Burkette, Allison, and William A. Kretzschmar, Jr. 2018. *Exploring Linguistic Science: Language Use, Complexity, and Interaction.* Cambridge: Cambridge University Press.

Butler, Judith. 1990. *Gender Trouble: Feminism and the Subversion of Identity.* New York: Routledge.

Charity Hudley, Anne H., Christine Mallinson, and Mary Bucholtz. 2020. "Toward Racial Justice in Linguistics: Interdisciplinary Insights into Theorizing Race in the Discipline and Diversifying the Profession." *Language* 96, no. 4 (Dec.): e200–235. https://doi.org/10.1353/lan.2020.0074.

Childs, Becky. 2021. "The Value of Interdisciplinary and Transdisciplinary Linguistic Research." In *Crossing Borders, Making Connections: Interdisciplinarity in Linguistics,* edited by Allison Burkette and Tamara Warhol, 7–21. Berlin: de Gruyter Mouton.

Cramer, Jennifer. 2016. *Contested Southerness: The Linguistic Production and Perception of Identity in the Borderlands.* Publication of the American Dialect Society 100. Durham, N.C.: Duke University Press. https://read.dukeupress.edu/pads/issue/100/1.

DeChants, Jonah P., Amy E. Green, Myeshia N. Price, and Carrie K. Davis. 2021. "Homelessness and Housing Instability among LGBTQ Youth." West Hollywood, Calif.: The Trevor Project. https://www.thetrevorproject.org/wp-content/uploads/2022/02/Trevor-Project-Homelessness-Report.pdf.

Dobrin, Lise M. and Jeff Good. 2009. "Practical Language Development: Whose Mission?" *Language* 85, no. 3 (Sept.): 619–29. https://doi.org/10.1353/lan.0.0152.

Fausto-Sterling, Anne. 2000. *Sexing the Body: Gender Politics and the Construction of Sexuality.* New York: Basic Books.

Grieser, Jessica A. 2022. *The Black Side of the River: Race, Language, and Belonging in Washington, DC.* Washington, D.C.: Georgetown University Press.

Halberstam, Judith. 2011. *The Queer Art of Failure.* Durham, N.C.: Duke University Press.

Halperin, David M. 1995. *Saint Foucault: Towards a Gay Hagiography.* New York: Oxford University Press.

Hernández, Ellie D., Eddy Francisco Alvarez Jr., and Magda García, eds. 2021. *Transmovimientos: Latinx Queer Migrations, Bodies, and Spaces.* Lincoln: University of Nebraska Press.

Kibbey, Tyler. 2019. "Transcriptivism: An Ethical Framework for Modern Linguistics." *Proceedings of the Linguistic Society of America* 4: art. 45. https://doi.org/10.3765/plsa.v4i1.4535.

Kibbey, Tyler. 2021. "Linguistics Out of the Closet: Comments on a Discipline's Anxiety." *Cadernos de Linguística* 2, no. 1: art. 293. https://doi.org/10.25189/2675-4916.2021.v2.n1.id293.

Kibbey, Tyler. Forthcoming. "The State of Tennessee and the Kingdom of God: Theo-Political Gender Ideology and the Emergence of Gender Transcendentalism in the American South." In *Linguistics Out of the Closet: The Interdisciplinarity of Gender and Sexuality in Language Science,* edited by Tyler Everett Kibbey. Berlin: Walter de Gruyter.

Kretzschmar, William A., Jr. 2015. *Language and Complex Systems.* Cambridge: Cambridge University Press.

Leap, William L., and Tom Boellstorff, eds. 2004. *Speaking in Queer Tongues: Globalization and Gay Language.* Urbana: University of Illinois Press.

Legman, Gershon. 1941. "The Language of Homosexuality: An American Glossary." In *Sex Variants: A Study of Homosexual Patterns,* edited by George W. Henry, 2: 1155–79. New York: P. Hoeber. Portion reprinted in *The Language and Sexuality Reader,* edited by Deborah Cameron and Don Kulick, 19–32. London: Routledge, 2006.

Levon, Erez. 2014. "Sexual Subjectivities and Lesbian and Gay Narratives of Belonging in Israel." In *Queer Excursions: Retheorizing Binaries in Language, Gender, and Sexuality,* edited by Lal Zimman, Jenny L. Davis, and Joshua Raclaw, 101–28. Oxford: Oxford University Press.

Luibhéid, Eithne, and Karma R. Chávez, eds. 2020. *Queer and Trans Migrations: Dynamics of Illegalization, Detention, and Deportation.* Urbana: University of Illinois Press.

Manion, Jen. 2020. *Female Husbands: A Trans History.* Cambridge: Cambridge University Press.

McCleary, Bryce. 2023. "'We All Country': Region, Place, and Community Language Among Oklahoma City Drag Performers." *American Speech* 98, no. 1 (Feb.): 11–39. https://doi.org/10.1215/00031283-10579442.

Miller, Merle. 1971. *On Being Different: What It Means to Be a Homosexual.* New York: Random House.

Queen, Robin. 2007. "Sociolinguistic Horizons: Language and Sexuality." *Language and Linguistic Compass* 1, no. 4 (July): 314–30. https://doi.org/10.1111/j.1749-818X.2007.00019.x.

Reed, Paul E. 2016. "Sounding Appalachian: /aɪ/ Monophthongization, Rising Pitch Accents, and Rootedness." Ph.D. diss., University of South Carolina.

Reed, Paul E. 2018. "Appalachia, Monopthongization, and Intonation: Rethinking Tradition." In *Language Variety in the New South: Contemporary Perspectives on Change and Variation,* edited by Jeffrey Reaser, Eric Wilbanks, Karissa Wojcik, and Walt Wolfram, 97–112. Chapel Hill: University of North Carolina Press.

Reed, Paul E. 2020a. "The Importance of Rootedness in the Study of Appalachian English: Case Study Evidence for a Proposed Rootedness Metric." *American Speech* 95, no. 2 (May): 203–26. https://doi.org/10.1215/00031283-7706532.

Reed, Paul E. 2020b. "Prosodic Variation and Rootedness in Appalachia English." In "Selected Papers from New Ways of Analyzing Variation (NWAV 47)," edited by Ruaridh Purse and Yosiane White. *University of Pennsylvania Working Papers in Linguistics* 25, no. 2: 107–14. https://repository.upenn.edu/pwpl/vol25/iss2/13/.

Sedgwick, Eve Kosofsky. 2008. *Epistemology of the Closet.* Berkeley: University of California Press.

van Klinken, Adriaan, Johanna Stiebert, Sebyala Brian, and Fredrick Hudson. 2021. *Sacred Queer Stories: Ugandan LGBTQ+ Refugee Lives and the Bible.* Woodbridge: James Currey Press.

Ward, Jane. 2015. *Not Gay: Sex Between Straight White Men.* New York: New York University Press.

Wolfram, Walt. 2015. "Sociolinguistic Engagement in Community Perspective." In *New Perspectives on Language Variety in the South: Historical and Contemporary Approaches,* edited by Michael D. Picone and Catherine Evans Davies, 731–47. Tuscaloosa: University of Alabama Press.

Wolfram, Walt, and Natalie Schilling-Estes. 1998. *American English: Dialects and Variation.* Malden, Mass.: Blackwell.

Zimman, Lal, Jenny L. Davis, and Joshua Raclaw, eds. 2014. *Queer Excursions: Retheorizing Binaries in Language, Gender, and Sexuality.* Oxford: Oxford University Press.

TYLER KIBBEY is a sociocognitive linguist working on issues surrounding language, religion, and violence. Tyler is currently a Ph.D. candidate in linguistics at Humboldt-Universität zu Berlin and a M.A./J.D. student in international law and diplomacy at the University of Kentucky. Email: tyler.e.kibbey@gmail.com.

AMONG THE NEW WORDS

BENJAMIN ZIMMER
Wall Street Journal

KELLY E. WRIGHT
Virginia Polytechnic Institute

BRIANNE HUGHES
Wordnik

LYNN ZHANG (张笛菲)
University of Wisconsin–Madison

JAIDAN McLEAN
University of Oregon

CHARLES E. CARSON
Duke University Press

Send newly found words to atnw@americandialect.org

For this special issue of *American Speech*, the ATNW editorial team chose to survey some recent developments in terminology across the broad category of gender and sexuality. This topic was most recently covered in our Winter 2014 installment (*AS* 89, no. 4: 470–96; https://doi .org/10.1215/00031283-2908233), which was inspired by the expanded options of sexual and gender identities made available by Facebook at the time. Since then, identity terms have further flourished as polls show more Americans identifying as LGBTQ and nonbinary (Morava and Andrew 2021).

To prepare for this installment, we sought out suggestions by crowdsourcing potential headwords by means of an online survey shared via the American Dialect Society's social media accounts. The survey offered a broad array of items across such categories as pronouns, identities, orientations, emoji, and Black Queer Femme culture. The survey also included a free space for additional suggestions. While some of our editorial team do proudly claim legibitiquois allegiance, none of us claim academic expertise in gender and sexuality; thus, the survey also allowed us to solicit suggestions for experts we should be in conversation with as this edition of ATNW developed.

We received enthusiastic engagement with these crowdsourcing efforts, eliciting 80 additional suggestions for headwords across categories from the 106 individuals who participated. These suggestions helped shape lively discussions among our editorial team and have reframed our long-term plans. For example, because Black Queer Femme contributions to the lexicon have been so rich and varied, we will be dedicating an upcoming edition solely to their coverage. Table 1 lists the candidate headwords in that category from the survey, just to whet readers' appetites. The most frequent

American Speech, Vol. 98, No. 1, February 2023   DOI 10.1215/00031283-10579494

TABLE 1

Frequent Black Queer Femme Terms from the ATNW Gender/Sexuality Survey

(it's) giving (life)	32	beat	12
clocked	26	painted	12
drag mother/mamma/momma	22	the fantasy	11
werk	20	three snaps	10
voguing	19	squirrelfriend	10
reading	19	kaikai	9
hanky codes	18	cakes	8

suggestion, *it's giving (X)* in the sense 'it's giving off a feeling/vibe/energy (of X)', won as ADS's 2022 Informal Word of Year and will be treated in our WOTY installment later this year.

After significant debate about the ways in which we could do justice to the remaining topics and in consultation with our guest experts for this issue, Kirby Conrod and Joshua Raclaw, we opted to preserve our traditional, alphabetical organization of this issue. The headwords chosen represent the top candidates in each of the survey categories mentioned, as well as some additional suggestions we received that our cadre of guest writers this edition will be highlighting.

This installment is not meant to be an exhaustive or comprehensive treatment of the terms related to gender and sexuality in our contemporary lexicon. The discursive entries we present here provide introductory overviews of lexical histories, not critical annotations of the concepts or histories the lexemes themselves describe, capture, engage, or resist.

Among the topics that are beyond the scope of our current treatment is the metalinguistic discourse surrounding personal pronoun choice, which has become highly politicized in recent years. The use of neopronouns as emblems of identity has been discussed previously in ATNW, such as our discussion in May 2016 installment (*AS* 91, no. 2; https://doi .org/10.1215/00031283-3633118) of "singular *they*," which was selected as the ADS Word of the Year in 2015 and subsequently as Word of the Decade at the society's 2020 meeting. *(My) pronouns* was selected as Word of the Year for 2019, as we discussed in February 2021 (*AS* 96, no. 1; https:// doi.org/10.1215/00031283-3442150). As Conrod (2022) has cogently argued, the word *pronouns* is very often used as a proxy for issues of trans identity in the ongoing culture wars, becoming little more than a dogwhistle in transphobic rhetoric. In this installment, we have chosen to focus on the linguistic use of communities of practice rather than the often bad-faith rhetorical deployment of terms like *pronouns*, recognizing the reality of these rhetorical uses and the harm they cause.

Furthermore, there are entire terrains of innovative usage that we cannot do justice in our limited space here. Neopronouns are a particularly fertile area of innovation, including such emerging phenomena as "noun-self pronouns" (Miltersen 2016; Marcus 2021), such as *fae/faer/faeself*, drawn from pagan and Celtic roots (Lodge 2021). The productivity of such novel forms deserves scholarly attention beyond what we can provide here.

In the treatments below we have also sought to explore terms that have not already received lexicographical treatment in other major reference works. The *Oxford English Dictionary* has in recent years greatly expanded its coverage of terms related to gender and sexuality, with recent additions to the online *OED* including *agender, ambisexual, aromantic, demisexual, genderfluid, non-binary,* and *trans** (Dent 2018; Watkins 2019). Several of these items also received earlier treatment in our 2014 exploration of gender and sexuality terms cited above. We have chosen here to focus on previously unexplored lexical developments; thus, instead of the already covered *aromantic,* we treat the clipping *aro* and related uses of the prefix *a-.*

As usual, each headword is provided with a paragraph-length discursive assessment, with full lexicographical treatments, including citational evidence, to be found in the online supplement for the electronic form of the journal. Supplementary material for this article is available at https://doi .org/10.1215/00031283-10579494.

Contributions of the coeditors of ATNW are identified by their initials: Benjamin Zimmer [BZ], Kelly E. Wright [KW], Brianne Hughes [BH], Jaidan McLean [JM], and Charles E. Carson [CC]. In addition, we are grateful for contributions to this installment from Archie Crowley (*T4T*), Brandon Sun Eagle Jent (*Two-Spirit*), Maureen Kosse (*birthing person*), and Jane Solomon (🐻 'pregnant person'). [KW and BZ]

THE WORDS

A-, ASPEC, ARO, AROACE. *Ace* (clipping of *asexual*) was covered in the previous ATNW on gender and sexuality (*AS* 89, no. 4 [Winter 2014]: 471–72), but the larger community has not yet been well-represented in major dictionaries. The default narrative in media is a will-they-won't-they sexual tension between two characters that inevitably kiss, partner up, and start a family. That assumption makes life hard for a demographic that does not desire all or any of those moments as life goals.

Asexual, aromantic, and asensual identities are real, their visibility is increasing, and their vocabulary is expanding. *Aspec* (or *a-spec*) has come to describe anyone who does not experience love and sexuality in that socially expected way. Whereas *ace* covers those with low or no sexual attraction, *aro* describes people with low or no interest in romantic relationships. People who experience both describe themselves as *aroace*.

Historically, the *a-* prefix negated whatever comes next, but as the aspec community has come into focus, *a-* terms can now be abbreviations for sexual and gender identities including agender, aflux (ace or aro with a fluctuation of attraction), and aplatonic. Aphobic people (modeled on *homophobic*) are not scared of nothingness; they are hateful toward aspec people and dehumanize them for not experiencing what they incorrectly assume is a core aspect of being alive. Ace and aspec erasure is also common in broader queer communities, where the *A* in *LGBTQIA+* is sometimes used to stand for *allies* instead of *ace* (see, e.g., Richard 2013).

The terms *a-spectrum, aspec, aroace*, and many others have all grown in use in the last 10 years through forums and blogging sites like Tumblr (e.g., HistoricallyAce 2017), not because aro and ace people are new, but because the internet has allowed previously isolated people to find community and discuss what it means to them to experience attraction and love and how it may change over time.

Aspec desires are often misunderstood or dismissed as a naive phase that will be solved when they meet "the right person." Thankfully, online communities have helped normalize aspec experiences, define the gray spectrum, and start deciding what an ideal life looks like for them. Some media now includes canon or implied aspec characters, including Todd Chavez from *Bojack Horseman* (Asexual Media Archives 2016; Cuby 2018), but it is still a seldom-recognized identity that is fought for by its members in their daily lives. Aspec is an umbrella term for a vast sea of human experience that is rarely legitimized and was not given labels until they identified it themselves. [BH]

ALLO-, ZED-. The pairing of the *cis-* and *trans-* prefixes has allowed for a reframing of identity terms relating to gender and sexuality, foregrounding that cisness (having a gender identity that matches the sex one was assigned at birth) is typically privileged as "unmarked" social category. A similar type of reframing has now led to the *allo-* prefix as the counterpart of *a-* as in *asexual* or *aromantic. Allo-* is derived from Greek ἄλλος 'other, another' and has been used as a scientific combining form since the nineteenth century. It does not necessarily pair as the opposite of *a-* in other cases; so, for instance, *allotheism* has been used historically in Christian contexts to mean 'worship of another god', while *theism* meaning 'belief in God' would pair as the opposite of *atheism* 'disbelief in God'. But in the case of romantic and sexual attraction, *allo-* has been pressed into service to describe 'someone who is attracted to another person', so that *alloromantic* opposes *aromantic* and *allosexual* opposes *asexual*. Perhaps due to the fact the *allo-* prefix is not semantically transparent to a general audience, a competing prefix has developed as an antonym for *a-*: *zed-*, which is understood in an alphabetic fashion, as in "from a to zed."

Regardless of whether *allo-* or *zed-* is the prefix used, it can stand as one end of a spectrum of attraction, so that *demisexual* or *graysexual* can describe middle points on a spectrum from *asexual* to *allosexual* or *zedsexual* (with *demiromantic/grayromantic* lying between the poles of *aromantic* and *alloromantic/zedromantic*). As with other prefixes considered here, *allo* and *zed* also have the potential to stand alone as free morphemes. [BZ]

BIRTHING PERSON. Discourse over the expression *birthing people* became mainstream in 2021, when Democratic Missouri Representative Cori Bush used the term while testifying before the Democratic Oversight Committee on the topic of Black pregnancy and birth care (Committee on Oversight and Accountability 2021). Later, she tweeted:

> Every day, Black birthing people and our babies die because our doctors don't believe our pain. My children almost became a statistic. I almost became a statistic. I testified about my experience @OversightDems today. Hear us. Believe us. Because for so long, nobody has. [Cori Bush (@RepCori), *Twitter*, May 6, 2021, https://twitter.com/RepCori/status/1390352127579594753]

Transgender people, especially transmasculine people, are often overlooked in discourses concerning pregnancy and childbirth. The term *birthing person*, alongside other expressions like *individuals with childbearing organs*, provides a gender-neutral alternative to words like *mother*, which may alienate pregnant people who are not women. The earliest reference to a birthing person in academic literature is a 2018 article in the *MIDIRS Midwifery Digest* (Hill and Firth 2018), a systematic review of factors which affect the wellbeing of pregnant people. Citing previous research on lesbian comothers, Hill and Firth stress the importance of respectful engagement with pregnant individuals to facilitate positive birth experiences: "Childbirth is one of the most important events in a person's life, with the experience being highly individual and transformative for each birthing person (BP). [...] With recognition of this highly individual experience, gender-neutral terminology will be used throughout this review to support inclusivity" (72). *Birthing person* has been adopted by many reproductive health organizations, providers, and doulas, as well as supporters of transgender rights (see 2023 Jan. 9 and 2023 Jan. 10 quots.). [Maureen Kosse]

GENDER EUPHORIA. Originating in contrast with the psychiatric term *gender dysphoria, gender euphoria* is a noun phrase used to describe the joyous feeling one has when experiencing something that affirms their gender identity. While the term *gender dysphoria* was first used by Norman Fisk in the 1970s, it is unclear where *gender euphoria* came from or who first used it (Beischel, Gauvin, and van Anders 2021). Jan Broekhuizen (2020), a transgender and nonbinary writer for *TRANS Magazine,* defines *gender euphoria* as "a feeling of well-being arising from affirmation of a person's gender." There is no one specific way to elicit gender euphoria, but rather it is a complex, nonlinear phenomenon that can be related to bodily attributes or social treatment from others. For example, presenting as the gender one identifies with or by using their correct pronouns, a transgender or nonbinary person can experience euphoria, an intense happiness and self-confidence, regarding their gender. In a YouTube video sharing lived experiences of gender euphoria, Aaron Ansuini relates a story from when he was a kid hitting puberty and used tape to bind himself, long before knowing what a binder was, yet experienced a sense of "I like that [...] I wish I looked like that all the time." Gender euphoria is a unique experience though, so at times it may be a moment of intense glee that accompanies a milestone in one's relationship with their gender identity, and at other times it's a more of calm relief in one's self (Jacobsen and Devor 2022). [JM]

NONBINARY. Although covered in the Winter 2014 installment of ATNW (*AS* 89, no. 4: 486–88) as an adjective, the term *nonbinary* (sometimes hyphenated, *non-binary*) calls for a 2023 update due to the evolution of its meaning from simply describing attributes that are neither feminine nor masculine to a term used in referring more specifically to one's gender identity. Some U.S. states have even adopted a nonbinary marker for use on government issued IDs, such as Oregon, where an *X* can be used in place of the binary *F* and *M* gender markers (O'Hara 2017). Although, when used in this way it may imply to some that nonbinary represents a sort of third gender, which GenderGP (2021) concisely refutes, "non-binary doesn't describe a single-gender identity so much as a vast range of identities that don't fit into a binary gender structure of male or female." A nonbinary person can relate one gender, more than one gender, no gender at all, or a fluidity between genders; *nonbinary* is used to describe a multitude of genders that don't fall in line with "male or female." The Nonbinary.wiki's definition of *nonbinary* notes how for some people this term is as specific as they'd prefer to be in labeling their gender, while others may specify an identity under the non-binary umbrella (https://nonbinary.wiki/wiki/Nonbinary).

Additionally, in considering this update of *nonbinary* as a term used to refer to someone's gender identity, it should be noted that the concept behind this usage has a long history. As many nonbinary discuss, from Charlie McNabb with their book *Nonbinary Gender Identities: History, Culture, Resources* (2017) to Kai (@mielaklv) on TikTok, the concept of the gender binary we hold today stems from colonization wherein non-White communities held nonbinary sexualities, identities, and customs that were conquered and replaced by the European notions of masculinity and femininity. This history of life beyond a gender binary can be traced to various non-White communities, such as the Anishinaabe Two Spirit people, the Hijras people in South Asia, and the Cook Islands' Akava'ine people. It is important to consider this history with how *nonbinary* is used today because it exemplifies that people can understand gender as a spectrum rather than a clear-cut binary, which is something necessary for referring to one's gender identity in the way the term is used today. [JM]

PAN. Sexual or romantic attraction to multiple genders has been called *bisexual* by psychologists since the early 1900s, then shortened to *bi* (*OED3* 1957–). When gender was understood as a binary—either man or woman—*bi* meant attraction to both. With increased visibility of nonbinary and trans identities, however, two no longer covers the infinite potential gender expressions in the world. In response to that, the term *pansexual* has grown in use for the last 20 years to explicitly indicate that someone is attracted to anyone, including trans and nonbinary people (Hinsliff 2019). *Pan* is a shortening for both *pansexual* and *panromantic*, depending on the context (someone could be both pan and aro or both pan and ace; see 2021 Sept. 20 quot., s.v. A-) Sometimes *bi* means *pan*, but *pan* never just means *bi*.

Pansexuality is not related to the god Pan, and pansexual people are not more likely to be polyamorous than any other orientation; they just have a wider pool of prospects. *Omnisexual* has also been coined (see 2012 June 8 quot.) to make a further distinction from *pan*, even though both roots mean 'all' in Latin and Greek, respectively. *Omni* can mean attraction to all genders, whereas *pan* can mean attraction regardless of gender, which is a useful distinction within the community. *Pan* is far more common, though, and often a standard inclusion in lists of sexual identities. [BH]

POLY. The related terms *polyamorous*, *polyamory*, and *polyamorist* all developed in the early 1990s to describe, as the *OED3* defines it, "the fact of having simultaneous close emotional relationships with two or more other individuals, viewed as an alternative to monogamy, esp. in regard to matters of sexual fidelity" or "the custom or practice of engaging in multiple sexual relationships with the knowledge and consent of all partners concerned" (s.v. *polyamory*). The usage found particular favor in online forums at the time, such as the Usenet newsgroup alt.polyamory, founded in 1992. In the FAQ document for the newsgroup, admin Elise Matthesen's (1997) definition of *polyamory* was kept intentionally loose: "Polyamory means 'loving more than one'. This love may be sexual, emotional, spiritual, or any combination thereof, according to the desires and agreements of the individuals involved, but you needn't wear yourself out trying to figure out ways to fit fondness for apple pie, or filial piety, or a passion for the Saint Paul Saints baseball club into it." The FAQ carried the caveat, "Some people think the definition is a bit loose, but it's got to be fairly roomy to fit the wide range of poly arrangements out there."

 Poly for *polyamorist* is dated by the *OED3* to 1992 (s.v. *poly*, n.[6]), while the same term can also refer to *polyamory* in citations starting from 2001 (s.v. *poly*, n.[7]). Since that time, the *poly-* prefix has spawned a number of related terms in the polyamory community, including *polycule*, which combines *polyamory* and *molecule* to denote all the members of a polyamorous group. *Polyfidelity*, meanwhile, is a polyamorous spin on the traditional notion of fidelity, where fidelity is to other members of a polyamorous group rather than to a single person. Other styles of polyamory now include solo polyamory, shortened to *solo poly*, in which a person may have multiple intimate relationships without cohabiting or "nesting" with any individual partner. Beyond these variations of polyamory lies what has been termed *relationship anarchy*, which applies anarchist principles to intimate relations, dispensing entirely with normative approaches to closeness and autonomy within relationships. [BZ]

🤰 (PREGNANT PERSON). 🤰 (pregnant man) and 🤰 (pregnant person) were approved in 2021 as part of Unicode 14.0 and started appearing on devices in late 2021/early 2022. The new pregnancy options may be used for representation by trans men, nonbinary people, or women with short hair—though, of course, use of these emoji is not limited to these groups. Its inclusion as part of the emoji set comes down to Unicode legacy decisions.

 To understand how 🤰 (pregnant man) and 🤰 (pregnant person) ended up as emoji, it's important to trace the evolution of gender in emoji from the very early days. The earliest emoji set on record is from 1997 and appeared on devices from the Japanese carrier SoftBank. It contains four explicitly gendered emoji: 👦 (boy), 👧 (girl), 👨 (man), and 👩 (woman). SoftBank's woman design from 1997 is just eyes, nose, and a mouth, which could represent a wide variety of people beyond just women. As more emoji are added, individual emoji tend to shift from semantic abstraction into specificity. This is exactly what has happened with the human emoji over the last two decades.

In 2019 Unicode established priorities to help improve emoji gender representation and to standardize inconsistencies in legacy decisions (Burge et al. 2019). Part of this is making sure all human emoji with a gender have a 'person', 'woman', and 'man' variant. The 'person' variant is supposed to be a gender-inclusive representation. Just as 'woman' emoji don't represent all women and 'man' emoji don't represent all men, 'person' emoji are an imperfect tool for representing all genders. Gender is not a haircut or an outfit. Emoji codepoints lack the nuance that exists in individuals. Accepting this as a limitation of emoji in general, Unicode's goal is to have more people feel represented via emoji.

Sometimes new gender variants of an emoji are added years after the original emoji was released. 🎅 (Mrs. Claus) and 🧑‍🎄 (Mx Claus), added in 2016 and 2020, respectively, fall into this category. So do 🫃 (pregnant man) and 🫄 (pregnant person). In her newsletter about the Emoji 14.0 release, chair of the Unicode Emoji Subcommittee Jennifer Daniel (2021), explains: "If the existing 'pregnant woman' had been named 'woman with swollen belly' these new emoji would've followed suit." Had 🤰 (pregnant woman) been approved in 2016 under a more descriptive name, we might be talking about the addition of "Man with Swollen Belly" and "Person with Swollen Belly" today instead of "Pregnant Man" and "Pregnant Person."

Naming conventions aside, men can be pregnant. This applies to the real world (e.g., trans men) and to fictional universes (e.g., Arnold Schwarzenegger in *Junior* and Lil Nas X's promotional materials for his album *Montero* [see 2021 Aug. 30 quot.]). People of any gender can be pregnant too and now there are emoji to represent this. [Jane Solomon]

ROLLING PRONOUNS; BILINGUAL PRONOUNS. Since they last graced our pages in February 2021 (*AS* 96, no. 1: 112–13), pronouns have become no less productive, used in all manner of gender-fuckery, empowering the *buns* and *innitselfs* out there. As documented then in our treatment of the 2019 WOTY *(my) pronouns*, many have begun engaging in the practice of marking publicly which pronouns they choose—such as *they/them/theirs*—either by posting them outside an office door, listing them in an email signature, or adding them on a social media profile. The sharing of pronouns in these kinds of public and digital spaces can be an act of meaning making in and of itself, with some trans and gender diverse individuals using that space as an early space for coming out with a newly adopted set of pronouns or as a way of signalling a position of allyship to those who break with cis-heteronormative understandings of gender (Raclaw et al. 2022). *Rolling pronouns* refer to those presented as options from multiple sets, such as *she/they*; because gender is a spectrum and people can feel like they have multiple genders or even no gender at a given point in time, using rolling pronouns allow for more comfort than choosing a singular set. Users may alternate between them or shift from one to the other over time (LGBTQ Nation 2022). As inclusivity efforts continue to expand, even this class of pronouns has become more productive, taking on neopronouns of its own in the Spanish *él* and *ella*. *Rolling bilingual pronouns*—which indicate not only multiple languages a person uses but also offer the potential for fluidity around the rigid gendered constructions their languages may present— *he/él* and *she/ella* have given users new ways to demonstrate the fullness of their identities (Rosen-Carroll 2022).

According to the 2020 Gender Census, when asked "which pronouns are you happy for people to use for you in English?," around half of the 24,576 adults surveyed chose two or more sets (Lodge 2020). This statistic reveals something that may be surprising to some readers; rolling pronouns aren't particularly new. In fact, as linguistic anthropologist Joshua Raclaw notes in the *Jewish Telegraphic Agency* (quoted in Hajdenberg 2022), Adam is referred to in the book of Genesis with both 'it' and 'them' Hebrew pronouns and that early rabbinical thought interprets this figure as both masculine and feminine. In recognition of this history, the widespead international adoption of rolling pronouns, as well as their uptake by celebrities like Halsey, Kehlani, and Rahul Kohli (López 2021), I suspect we'll see this class continue to grow and change for some time. So watch this space! [KW]

T4T. *T4t* began as an abbreviation of *trans for trans* and has come to represent an orientation to care and love between trans individuals and communities. The term originated in the early 2000s as a category on the Craigslist personals, which listed abbreviations such as *m4m* 'male for male' and *m4t* 'male for trans' to allow users to find connections for dating and hookups. *T4t* functioned as a way to separate trans people from the *m*s and *w*s, yet also provided a place for trans people to connect with each other. In 2018, the Online Sex Trafficking Act (FOSTA) and the Stop Enabling Sex Traffickers Act (SESTA) resulted in the dissolution of the personal ads section of Craigslist (Williams 2018). Despite the section's removal, *t4t* was taken up on other social media sites, primarily as a hashtag, where *#t4t* was used to share pictures of trans couples, content related to the experience of dating another trans person, and memes. One meme from a now-defunct instagram account, @bannedtrans, featured a photo of a pharmacy line with a large *#T4T* accompanied by the text "what if we kissed in the line to get our hormones at the CVS pharmacy???" (see 2019 Dec. 18 quot.). This use of *t4t* highlighted the benefits of sharing the mundane aspects of trans life, such as picking up hormones with another trans person. As *t4t* usage became more common, it appeared without the hash mark. Uses of *t4t* were both playful in reference to trans relationships and serious in their considerations of movements for trans justice: "that t4t shit heals ur soul, makes you see the pearly gates and shit, god fucking bless" (see 2022 Oct. 8 quot.). Further, *t4t* tattoos gained popularity as a physical embodiment of trans solidarity (Woodstock 2022; see Nov 13, 2022). The term has been taken up in academic theorizing about trans life, as demonstrated by the May 2021 *Transgender Studies Quarterly* issue centered on *t4t* (Awkward-Rich and Malatino 2022). T4t has become a shorthand for larger discourses within the trans community regarding the political radicality of transgender love and desirability outside of the cisgender gaze as well as possibilities for healing, support, and love. [Archie Crowley]

▬ (TRANSGENDER FLAG). To understand how we came to have a trangender flag emoji—its etymology, if you will—we need to go back to the late 1970s, when flags were first embraced by the gay liberation movement as a mean to express identity and solidarity. Feeling that the pink triangle used early in the movement had some dark baggage (i.e., Nazis), activists wanted a new symbol and tasked artist Gilbert Baker with its creation. Given the preponderance of identity flags today, a new flag design seems an obvious choice, but at that time, flags were used primarily to express regional or institutional affiliation. As Baker (2019, 36) notes in his memoir: "In the past, when I had thought of a flag, I saw it as just another icon to lampoon. I had considered all flag-waving and patriotism in general to be a dangerous joke. […] After the orgy of bunting and hoopla surrounding the Bicentennial [in 1976], I thought of flags in a new light. I discovered the depth of their power, their transcendent, transformative quality." The rainbow, he writes, was inspired by the diverse crowd of people dancing at the Winterland Ballroom: "We were all in a swirl of color and light. It was like a rainbow."

So why have so many groups under that rainbow umbrella produced their own flags given that the design was intended to represent the spectrum of the LGBTQ+ community? Well, because it wasn't. Gay liberation at the time was about the Ls, Gs, and sometimes Bs, that is, about sexual orientation but firmly cis and binary. Thus, a distinctive bisexual pride flag, designed by Michael Page in 1998, was the first analogous design to appear, quickly followed by the transgender pride flag, designed by Monica Helms in 1999, and many more.

With dozens of flags representing different variations of sexual orientation and gender expression, why are only two available as emoji, ▬ and ▬? Since emoji escaped their native Japan in 2008, the introduction of new emoji has been decided by a special committee of the Unicode Consortium, the international standardizing body that maintains the coding standard that includes all the world's writing systems. Based on feedback from tech companies and other interested parties, the committee established objective criteria, which the other flags have failed to meet. In fact, the trans pride flag was also rejected the first few times it was proposed, but it was eventually approved in 2019, in part because a few apps (Skype and WhatsApp) hadn't waited and had already incorporated it. And since compatibility across operating systems and apps is Unicode's primary goal, the scale was tipped in its favor. (In 2018, when an earlier proposal for a trans pride flag emoji had been rejected, activists attempted to hijack the lobster emoji as a trans pride symbol in protest, choosing it from that year's set of approved emoji in part because lobsters can display gynandromorphic characteristics [Lang 2018].) However, just because it now appears in the Unicode Standard does not mean that all OSs and apps need support it. If for some reason it's not supported, either because of developer opted not to or the device or program predates the emoji's existence, it appears as ▭▯.

So now that it's been approved, how is the trans flag emoji being used? It's still too new to show up meaningfully in frequency data, but the rainbow flag ranks 377 out of around 1,500 emoji (Daniel 2019). It's most often used in user names and profiles on social media (e.g., "Catherine McKenney ▬ (they/them)") and as a way to tag posts about trans pride events and commemorations (e.g., "Happy Pride Month! ▬▬"). Occasionally, the emoji is also found in rebuses in place of the syllable *trans*, as in "▬phobia" and "lost in ▬lation" [CC]

TWO-SPIRIT. *Two-Spirit* refers to the various gender roles, gender expressions, and sexual orientations that are interwoven with traditional gender, ceremony, and broader social systems of Indigenous societies. It was first revealed in a dream to Anishinaabe elder Myra Laramee and later adopted by attendees of the third International Gathering of American Indian and First Nation Gays and Lesbians, August 1990, in Winnipeg, Manitoba (City of Winnipeg 2021; Smithers 2022). A calque of the Anishinaabemowin (Ojibwe) term *niizh manidoowag, Two-Spirit* "expresses the existence of feminine and masculine qualities in a single person" (Smithers 2022, 189). While it is generally agreed upon that *Two-Spirit* is a useful placeholder in English, Two-Spirited people also assert its limitations. As Delaronde

(2021) notes, "It is impossible to define Two-Spirit in a singular sentence, or in a simplified way that would only strip such a purposefully nuanced and flexible term of all its power. Even to call Two-Spirit inherently queer would be a gross misunderstanding of all the ways the identity can manifest and be understood by the people who belong to it." Given that *Two-Spirit* refers to identities that exist outside of colonial logic (Driskill 2016) but lacks the myriad social, cultural, and linguistic contexts in which Two-Spirit identities are formed and understood, the term does not fully capture the dynamism of Two-Spirit ways of being. Below are examples of terms for Two-Spirit identities as they appear in Indigenous languages across Turtle Island (North America) and Abya Yala (The Americas):

> ᎦᏩᏯ (Tsalagi/Cherokee): ᎠᏎᎩ ᎠᏓᏅᏙ *asegi adanvdo* 'strange heart/spirit'
> Diné Bizaad (Navajo): *nádleehí* 'one who becomes/transforms/changes'
> Shiwi'ma (Zuni): *lhamana*, denoting third gender category
> Dille'xhonh (Zapotec): *muxe*, from Spanish *mujer* 'woman', denoting third
>   gender category
> 'Ōlelo Hawai'i (Hawaiian): *māhū* 'the in-between'
> Mapuzungun (Mapuche) *machi*, healer and religious leader
>   (see Bacigalupo 2007, 2016)

See also Lo Vecchio's (2022) discussion of Indigenous North Americans' rejection of *bedache* in favor of *Two-Spirit* and Elchacar's (2023 [this issue]) discussion of *two-spirit* and *bispirituel* in Quebec French. [Brandon Sun Eagle Jent]

REFERENCES

References to dated quotations (e.g., "see 2018 Sept. 9 quot.") refer to citations in the full lexicographical treatments, available online as supplemental material (https://doi.org/10.1215/00031283-10579494).

Asexual Media Archives. 2016. "BoJack Horseman S03E12—Todd Chavez comes out as asexual—22 July 2016." *YouTube*, Oct. 23, 2016. https://www.youtube.com/watch?v=Neo4O7X4Lic.

Asuini, Aaron. 2018. "Gender Dysphoria vs Gender EUPHORIA, ft. Ash Hardell!!" *YouTube*, Apr. 13, 2018. https://www.youtube.com/watch?v=HnkrhYAkWPs.

Awkward-Rich, Cameron, and Hil Malatino, eds. 2022. "The t4t Issue." Special issue, *TSQ: Transgender Studies Quarterly* 9, no. 1 (Feb.). https://read.dukeupress.edu/tsq/issue/9/1.

Bacigalupo, Ana Mariella. 2007. *Shamans of the Foye Tree: Gender, Power, and Healing among Chilean Mapuche*. Austin: University of Texas Press.

Bacigalupo, Ana Mariella. 2016. *Thunder Shaman: Making History with Mapuche Spirits in Chile and Patagonia*. Austin: University of Texas Press.

Baker, Gilbert. 2019. *Rainbow Warrior: My Life in Color*. Chicago: Chicago Review Press.

Beischel, Will J., Stéphanie E. M. Gauvin, and Sari M. van Anders. 2021. "'A Little Shiny Gender Breakthrough': Community Understandings of Gender Euphoria." *International Journal of Transgender Health* 23, no. 3 (May): 274–94. https://www.ncbi.nlm.nih.gov/pmc/articles/PMC9255216/.

Broekhuizen, Jan. 2020. "10 Reasons to Envy Trans People." *TRANS Magazine*, July 20, 2020. https://transmagazine.nl/gender-euphoria/.

Burge, Jeremy, and the Emoji Subcommittee. 2019. "Priorities for Future RGI Emoji Sequences." Unicode Consortium. Document L2/19-101. https://www.unicode.org/L2/L2019/19101-esc-rgi-priorities.pdf.

City of Winnipeg. 2021. "Two-Spirit—A Movement Born in Winnipeg." YouTube, Sept. 7, 2021. https://www.youtube.com/watch?v=Eu4xNUq2hGE.

Committee on Oversight and Accountability. 2021. "Oversight Committee Held Landmark Hearing Examining America's Black Maternal Health Crisis." U.S. House of Representatives. Press release, May 7, 2021. https://oversightdemocrats.house.gov/news/press-releases/oversight-committee-held-landmark-hearing-examining-america-s-black-maternal.

Conrod, Kirby. 2022. "The Right Doesn't Care What a Pronoun Is." *Medium*, Sept. 22, 2022. https://kconrod.medium.com/the-right-doesnt-care-what-a-pronoun-is-540cc4cab79d.

Cuby, Michael. 2018. "Why I Find *BoJack Horseman*'s Depiction of Asexuality Deeply Relatable." *Them*, Sept. 26, 2018. https://www.them.us/story/bojack-horseman-asexuality.

Daniel, Jennifer. 2019. "The Most Frequently Used Emoji in 2021." Unicode Consortium, Dec. 21, 2019. https://home.unicode.org/emoji/emoji-frequency/.

Daniel, Jennifer. 2021. "Did Someone Say New Emoji????" *Did Someone Say Emoji?* (blog). *Substack*, Sept. 14, 2021. https://jenniferdaniel.substack.com/p/did-someone-say-new-emoji.

Delaronde, Diikahnéhi Akwiráes. 2021. "So You Think You're Two-Spirit? (You're Wrong)." *Queer Kentucky*, Nov. 5, 2021. https://queerkentucky.com/so-you-think-youre-two-spirit-youre-wrong/.

Dent, Jonathan. 2018. "Release Notes: The Formal Language of Sexuality and Gender Identity." *Oxford English Dictionary* blog, Mar. 29, 2018. https://public.oed.com/blog/march-2018-update-release-notes-formal-language-sexuality-gender-identity/.

Driskill, Qwo-Li. 2016. *Asegi Stories: Cherokee Queer and Two-Spirit Memory.* Tucson: University of Arizona Press.

Elchacar, Mireille. 2023. "The Influence of English on Neologisms for Nonbinary Gender Identities and Sexual Orientations in Quebec French: Between Variation and Purism." In "Queer and Trans Dialectology: Exploring the Intersectionality of Regionality," edited by Bryce McCleary and Tyler Kibbee. Special issue, *American Speech* 98, no. 1 (Feb.): 40–66. https://doi.org/10.1215/00031283-10579455.

GenderGP. 2021. "Non-Binary People in History: Why Aren't They Recognised?" *GenderGP*, July 12, 2021. https://www.gendergp.com/non-binary-people-in-history/.

Hajdenberg, Jackie. 2022. "Non-gendered Language for Calling Jews to the Torah Gets Conservative Movement Approval." Jewish Telegraphic Agency, June 8, 2022. https://www.jta.org/2022/06/08/religion/non-gendered-language-for-calling-jews-to-the-torah-gets-conservative-movement-signoff.

Hill, Emily, and Amanda Firth. 2018. "Positive Birth Experiences: A Systematic Review of the Lived Experience from a Birthing Person's Perspective." *MIDIRS Midwifery Digest* 28, no. 1 (Mar.): 71–78. http://hdl.handle.net/10454/14860.

Hinsliff, Gaby. 2019. "The Pansexual Revolution: How Sexual Fluidity Became Mainstream." *Guardian*, Feb. 14, 2019. https://www.theguardian.com/society/2019/feb/14/the-pansexual-revolution-how-sexual-fluidity-became-mainstream.

HistoricallyAce. 2017. "Do you, per chance, know when asexuals first started using the term 'aspec'?" *Aceing History* (blog). *Tumblr*, June 6, 2017. https://historicallyace.tumblr.com/post/161502315942/do-you-per-chance-know-when-asexuals-first.

Jacobsen, Kai, and Aaron Devor. 2022. "Moving from Gender Dysphoria to Gender Euphoria: Trans Experiences of Positive Gender-Related Emotions." *Bulletin of Applied Transgender Studies* 1, nos. 1–2 (June): 119–43. https://bulletin.applied transstudies.org/article/1/1-2/6/.

Kai (@mielaklv). 2021. "non-binary. #SwitchTheChobaniFlip #fyp #nonbinary #non binarytiktok #lgbtq #typing." *TikTok*, Jan. 27, 2021. https://www.tiktok.com/@mielaklv/video/6922520990706568453.

Lang, Cady. 2018. "Here's Why People Are Using the Lobster Emoji to Rally for Transgender Representation." *Time*, Aug. 13, 2018. https://time.com/5365725/lobster-emoji-trans-representation/.

LGBTQ Nation. 2022. "Why Some People Use she/they & he/they Pronouns." May 30, 2022. https://www.lgbtqnation.com/2022/05/people-use-pronouns/.

[Lodge, Cassian]. 2020. "Gender Census 2020: Worldwide Report." Gender Census, Nov. 2, 2020. https://www.gendercensus.com/results/2020-worldwide/.

[Lodge, Cassian]. 2021. "On fae/faer Pronouns and Cultural Appropriation." *Gender Census* (blog). *Tumblr*, Feb. 20, 2021. https://gendercensus.tumblr.com/post/643657043304153088/on-faefaer-pronouns-and-cultural-appropriation.

López, Quispe. 2021. "12 Celebrities Who Use Rolling Gender Pronouns." *Insider*, Nov. 30, 2021. https://www.insider.com/celebrities-who-use-rolling-gender-pronouns-2021-9.

Lo Vecchio, Nicholas. 2022. "Revisiting *berdache*: Notes on a Transatlantic Lexical Creation." *American Speech* 97, no. 3 (Aug.): 345–73. https://doi.org/10.1215/00031283-9616142.

Marcus, Ezra. 2021. "A Guide to Neopronouns." *New York Times*, Apr. 8, 2021. https://www.nytimes.com/2021/04/08/style/neopronouns-nonbinary-explainer.html.

Matthesen, Elise. 1997. "alt.polyamory Frequently Asked Questions (FAQ)." *alt.polyamory* (newsgroup). *Usenet*, June 10, 1997. https://web.archive.org/web/19970808170207/http://www.faqs.org/faqs/polyamory/faq/.

McNabb, Charlie. 2017. *Nonbinary Gender Identities: History, Culture, Resources.* Lanham, Md.: Rowman and Littlefield.

Miltersen, Ehm Hjorth. 2016. "Nounself Pronouns: 3rd Person Personal Pronouns as Identity Expression." *Journal of Language Works / Sprogvidenskabeligt Studentertidsskrift* 1: 37–62. https://tidsskrift.dk/lwo/article/view/23431.

Morava, Maria, and Scottie Andrew. 2021. "More Americans Are Identifying as LGBTQ than Ever Before, Poll Finds." CNN, Feb 24. https://www.cnn.com/2021/02/24/us/americans-identifying-lgbtq-poll-trnd/index.html.

OED Online. 2000–. Oxford University Press. https://www.oed.com/. Originally based on the *Oxford English Dictionary*, 2nd ed. (1989); incrementally revised in preparation for 3rd ed.

O'Hara, Mary Emily. 2017. "Oregon Becomes First State to Add Third Gender to Driver's Licenses." *NBC News*, June 15, 2017. https://www.nbcnews.com/feature/nbc-out/oregon-becomes-first-state-add-third-gender-driver-s-licenses-n772891.

Raclaw, Joshua, Tommy Johnston, Olivia Marquardt, and Veronica Nazarewycz. 2022. "'Can I Be Genderqueer *and* a Woman?': Beyond the Binary in Gender and Pronoun Use." Paper presented at the Feminist Research Soireé, Women's and Gender Studies Dept., West Chester University, Oct. 27, 2022.

Richard, Katherine. 2013. "'A' Stands for Asexuals and Not Allies." *The Maroon* (Loyola University), Sept. 5, 2013. https://loyolamaroon.com/102130/oped/opinions/column-a-stands-for-asexuals-and-not-allies/.

Rossen-Carroll, Rachel. 2022. "What Are Él, Ella, and Elle Pronouns? And What Does 'Latinx' Really Mean?" *Interact*, Oct. 27, 2022. https://interactcom.com/what-are-el-ella-and-elle-pronouns-and-what-does-latinx-really-mean-hispanic-heritage-month-roundup/.

Smithers, Gregory D. 2022. *Reclaiming Two-Spirit: Sexuality, Spiritial Renewal, and Sovereignty in Native America*. Boston: Beacon Press.

Watkins, Susan. 2019. "Gender and Genre: Students, Researchers, and the OED." *Oxford English Dictionary* blog, Feb. 17, 2019. https://public.oed.com/blog/gender-and-genre-students-researchers-and-the-oed/.

Williams, Rachel Anne. 2018. "t4t and Trans Separatism: The Politic of Radical Love." *Medium*, Apr. 4, 2018. https://medium.com/@transphilosophr/t4t-and-the-micropolitics-of-trans-liberation-357df39df017.

Woodstock, Tuck. 2021. "Torrey Peters." *Gender Reveal* (podcast), ep. 91, Mar. 15, 2021. https://podcasts.apple.com/us/podcast/torrey-peters/id1330522019?i=1000513042963.

Keep up to date on new scholarship

Issue alerts are a great way to stay current on all the cutting-edge scholarship from your favorite Duke University Press journals. This free service delivers tables of contents directly to your inbox, informing you of the latest groundbreaking work as soon as it is published.

To sign up for issue alerts:

1. Visit **dukeu.press/register** and register for an account. You do not need to provide a customer number.

2. After registering, visit **dukeu.press/alerts**.

3. Go to "Latest Issue Alerts" and click on "Add Alerts."

4. Select as many publications as you would like from the pop-up window and click "Add Alerts."

read.dukeupress.edu/journals